THE TEN SMARTEST DECISIONS A WOMAN CAN MAKE AFTER FORTY

Tina B. Tessina, Ph.D.

RENAISSANCE BOOKS

Los Angeles

To the women:
Maggie, Sylvia, Isadora, Joan, Victoria, Carrie, Deni, Bonnie, Robin.
My companions and friends of many years,
my source of walking buddies, listening ears,
comfort, laughter, camaraderie, and joy.
And to the new generation, Amanda and Helia

Life is fun because of you.

Passages from Csikszentmihalyi, Mihaly, *Flow: The Psychology of Optimal Experience;* Moore, Thomas, *Care of the Soul;* Ornish, Dean, M.D, *Love and Survival: The Scientific Basis for the Healing Power of Intimacy;* Roizen, Michael, *Real Age: Are You as Young as You Can Be?;* Siegel, Bernie, M.D, *Peace, Love and Healing;* reprinted with permission from HarperCollins Publishers, Inc.

Library of Congress Cataloging-in-Publication Data
Tessina, Tina B.
    The ten smartest decisions a woman can make after forty / Tina B. Tessina.
        p. cm.
    Includes bibliographical references and index.
    ISBN 1-58063-181-9
        1. Middle aged women—Life skills guides. 2. Middle aged women—Psychology.
3. Decision making. 4. Self-actualization (Psychology) in middle age. I. Title.
HQ1059.4.T47 2001
646.7'0084'4—dc21   00-051717

10 9 8 7 6 5 4 3 2 1

Design by Jesús Arellano

Published by Renaissance Books
Distributed by St. Martin's Press
Manufactured in the United States of America
First edition

ACKNOWLEDGMENTS

No book is ever written without a tremendous amount of help, and I have many people to thank:

First and foremost, Laurie Harper, my agent, who has been a godsend, and who fights for me all the way. Laurie, you're a marvel.

Dick O'Connor and Michael Dougherty of Renaissance Books. I am so glad to be working again with you and to have such experts for friends.

Amanda Pisani, for her clear editorial eye and forthright approach. Lisa Lenthall and Jesús Arellano for their outstanding design.

My secretary, Ruth Campbell, who has been with me for years—patient, painstaking, willing, and reliable.

My beloved Richard, husband and best friend, who patiently suffers neglect whenever I'm writing. I'm a fortunate woman to have a husband so supportive, flexible, and so obviously loving. My love, what a treasure you are!

The tremendous resource of writers that is ASJA—someone there always has the answer.

When close family is all gone, in the end it's friends who support, encourage, love, and keep me loving life and really grateful for them: all the women in the dedication, plus Eddie Bialack David Groves, Glen McWilliams, Bill Mueller, and Riley K. Smith (meet you for tea at Beverly's Vintage Tea Leaf or lunch at Cindy's The Coffee Cup).

CONTENTS

Maturity:
The Freedom to Decide

And then, not expecting it, you become middle-aged . . . You achieve a wonderful freedom. It is a positive thing.

—Doris Lessing

A round the age of forty, we develop a new set of expectations. Forty represents midlife. Psychologists generally use the phrase "midlife crisis" to describe a period experienced by men. As depicted in popular culture, the midlife crisis male will often develop a need to buy an expensive car and leave his wife for a younger woman. But what of women? Women who are afraid of aging approach forty with dread, but many women, who have devoted their lives to raising children and caring for others, or who have focused on making a success of their careers, secretly see forty as a new opportunity. At forty it is possible to view life from a new perspective. You have goals and aspirations yet to achieve, but you also realize that you're not getting younger. Forty is a time for readjusting your focus, and for getting your whole act together. If you do, you'll remove the fear that comes with passing forty, and open a new vista of freedom and opportunity for yourself.

The majority of women enter perimenopause (the beginning of the hormonal changes leading to full menopause) by age forty-five, and at forty many women begin to wonder what menopause will bring. Unless you're one of the few women who plan to take advantage of recent medical developments that allow older women to carry *in vitro* fertilization babies to term, the opportunity to have children and the responsibilities of becoming a parent are dwindling.

LIVING IN A CHANGING SOCIETY

Women in midlife have always undergone physical changes, but women in our modern society must cope with social changes as well. In our brave age of technology and mobility, women over forty have, willingly or not, been pioneers of social and technological change. More educated than their mothers and grandmothers, most women over forty have work histories outside the home, and many have careers their forebears never dreamed possible. As a forty-something woman today, you have a lot of life experience, including experience in making your own decisions and the heavy responsibility that comes with that. You may be a single parent, self-employed, or a successful professional: someone who is forward-thinking and up-to-date with the technology. You have made decisions all your life, so why would you need a book like this one? Because decisionmaking is not easy for anyone, regardless of her history. I've been working with thousands of women of all ages for twenty-five years—I've taught college classes, treated clients in therapy, given lectures, and conducted workshops. In my work, one of the most frequent questions I am asked is, "How can I trust that my decisions are good ones?"

In *The 10 Smartest Decisions a Woman Can Make Before 40,* I wrote:

> Even the most educated and aware people often hesitate when making both long-term and short-term decisions, and many more are very uncomfortable being decisive at all. Much has been written about the pressures put on men, leading to stress, burnout, heart attacks and other physical and emotional problems. Less is heard about how difficult decision-making can be for today's women. With new technology and conveniences, life is lived at a faster pace than it was for previous generations and it is much more complex than it was for our grandparents, or even our parents.

This is equally true for the woman over forty.

Most of the women you knew as a child, including your mother, expected to be wives and mothers when they reached adulthood. These were the women's roles projected by our culture. Yet most mature women today have had children and careers. In fact, women forty and over have been in high-stress, demanding situations most of their adult lives. Somewhere between childhood and growing up, all the rules were changed!

At forty you have an opportunity to rethink your priorities. If you have children, most likely they are growing up and no longer need you as much as they once did. You have been working long enough to feel settled and experienced in your career, and you probably can see, in your aging parents and relatives, that there will be a time when you won't have the ability and opportunity that you do now. If you are like the over-forty women I see in my practice, you are longing to express the parts of yourself that have been neglected or ignored. Reaching forty means asking: What is my life about? Is my career gratifying enough? How am I going to feel when I reach old age? Will I be satisfied with what I've done? These questions require a new kind of decision-making expertise.

YOU CAN'T PREDICT THE FUTURE

If there's one thing life has taught you, it's that the future is impossible to predict. As you pass through each stage of life, your experiences continue to be new, and your roles and relationships keep changing. Life is in constant flux, and as soon as you feel you've mastered a role, a job, or a relationship, something shifts and you need to re-decide.

If you have been single until now, focused on your career and friends, traveling all over, you may be longing to be settled and close to your family. If you have been a single parent, and your children are growing up, you may be feeling a new kind of freedom. If you're married and working, you may be planning for and looking forward to your retirement. If circumstances have been difficult, perhaps the idea of retirement produces anxiety—it may be time to reorganize your relationship to your money and your future. All of these changes require new, smart decisions—perhaps of a kind you never before considered.

In your lifetime, you have gone from dial telephones to cell phones, Instant Messaging on the Internet, and shopping on the Web. In the workplace, jobs that require travel, permit telecommuting, and working on laptop computers are becoming commonplace. Keeping up with the rapid pace of change we live in today (perhaps even defending yourself from it) requires a new kind of decision-making.

In addition to keeping up with the technological evolution, you have responsibilities to meet at home, on the job, and in your personal life. If you feel overwhelmed at times, and find that you simply can't find the time to devote to looking at the big picture, you are not alone. By focusing on the day-to-day details, you forget to plan ahead, to anticipate change, and before you realize it, some neglected aspect of your personal or family life is in crisis.

It's time to stop briefly and take a look at where you are at this midpoint of your life span. If you follow the advice in the upcoming chapters, and spend a few productive hours evaluating where you are and where you're headed, you can create a much more satisfying, productive, and fulfilling future for yourself and for those you love.

Successfully re-creating your life at this point involves several crucial factors:

1. FUTURE SECURITY. Planning a secure future for yourself, if you have not done so already, is essential now. This, as we will see in chapter 6, involves getting appropriate financial advice and managing your money, something women "of a certain age" often feel unprepared for. But money isn't the whole picture. Making sure your lifestyle, habits, and attitudes are consistent

with maintaining your personal health and well-being is crucial to making the coming years feel like a reward for all your hard work. The information and examples provided here will help you make effective choices for your future security.

2. CHANGING ROLES. About this time in your life you see shifts in your family's needs. The generation following you is growing up, and the generation before you is getting older. Your own generation has reached the point of maximum responsibility. Many women find that just as they are being relieved of some of the responsibility for their children, they are taking on the burden of caring for aging parents or grandparents. Both of these factors impact your family decisions and your personal life in profound ways. In the coming pages you'll find guidelines and exercises that will help you manage these new responsibilities successfully and effectively, keeping your life in balance, or perhaps achieving that balance for the first time.

3. SATISFACTION. After many years of being a responsible, hardworking adult and (for many women) focusing on taking care of others at home, at work, and in family relationships, many women find that they don't know what they want for themselves. It's time to learn how to make the decisions that create the enriched, satisfying experience you always hoped your life would be. In this book you'll discover what satisfaction means for you, and how to refocus your life to create more of it.

4. ENJOYMENT. Your ability to take pleasure in life, to "lighten up," to find the fun in a simple moment, may have been suppressed

over the years. For some women, reconnecting with their lighthearted selves may simply require an attitude change; for others it requires major decisions to simplify and reshape their goals. For you, it could be some combination. In the following chapters you'll learn how to make the decisions that free you up to have more fun.

SMART DECISIONS FOR WOMEN OVER FORTY

If you stop to think about it, you know the difference between the women who make smart, considered decisions, and those who seem to let life push them around. You probably know people who succeed despite difficulties and bad breaks, and people who seem to have everything handed to them, but still can't get it together. You know people whose lives seem full of satisfaction and accomplishment, and others who don't feel that they have achieved anything worthwhile. Their lives are full of regret and complaints.

When life presents new challenges some people adapt quickly, yet others seem more comfortable staying "stuck" in familiar roles and familiar activities. Some women seem to know exactly what they want to do, regardless of their circumstances, and some can't seem to find a direction.

Do you know women who prefer to let others make their decisions for them? They follow the advice of their spouse or other family member, just doing what is expected of them. How happy and satisfied do you think they are? What happens when no one is around to "take care of things" anymore? Cooperating and being congenial with the people you care about makes your relationships run more smoothly (at least on the surface). However, when you relinquish your power to decide for yourself, your self-esteem suffers, and you feel out of control and unimportant, even in your own life.

As you reflect on the people you know, can you see the difference between the women who know how to make good decisions, and those who aren't sure what to do? None of us is completely confident with every decision we need to make in life, but those who understand that their decisions will create their outcome, and who consider carefully the outcome that they want to create, feel more secure more of the time.

As a woman over forty, you are entering a time of greater freedom and greater responsibility toward yourself. As the years pass and circumstances change, your accustomed role in life changes also. You will probably be needed less by your children, will have more responsibility for aging parents, and will be more aware of the passing of time. You may also feel more isolated, overwhelmed, and alienated.

You may find that your work, which was once enjoyable, is now less satisfying. Perhaps you have mastered it and done it long enough that you're a bit burnt-out or bored. You may even long to pass your hard-won skills on to others, to teach what you know.

Because you've lived long enough to master the basic skills of life, you may be wondering what else there is. For many women in midlife, going through days focused on material things and daily chores no longer seems sufficient. At this point many women begin to search for a different kind of meaning. "What is my life about?" they ask. "I have most everything I want. Why doesn't it feel like enough?"

In my therapy practice, these are the questions mature women ask and the forces behind the decisions they must learn to make. Understanding the important issues of this phase of your life, and being prepared to reevaluate your goals, find meaning, and make new kinds of decisions are the tasks you face now. How you meet these challenges will make the difference in how satisfying and rewarding the rest of your life will be. From experience, you know you cannot control everything that happens to you. But you can control your reactions and responses to the events around you. If you can think clearly despite changes, surprises, and unplanned circumstances, and you know how to make good choices and decisions, you will succeed in all the ways you want.

You can reorganize and restructure your goals to take care of yourself physically, emotionally, financially, and socially, no matter what your life circumstances have brought you. This is your opportunity to make the most of your life, to bring long-awaited dreams into reality, and to create meaning and satisfaction for yourself.

CREATE YOUR OWN STANDARDS

In spite of the many achievements of women in our culture, we are still evaluated by our appearance more often than by our accomplishments. When a woman in the public eye manages to be both attractive and effective, the positive commentary about her always seems to be how great she looks, not how big her stock portfolio is or how well she runs her company. Oprah's weight fluctuations and her cover photo for *Vogue* have garnered far more media attention than her amazing business accomplishments. Examples of spiritual achievements and an exemplary life are even less visible unless, as with Princess Diana, they come as a package with glamour, wealth, and fame, or the saintliness of Mother Teresa. The only qualities that seem to be valued these days are the ones that play well on TV.

Making smart, effective decisions about your own life depends on learning to set your own standards according to the values that work for you, rather than imitating the questionable and often contradictory values the media provides. At the same time, observing those around you is a great way to see how various value systems work and can offer you guidance in defining your own standards.

Role Models from Real Life

The most instructive lives to learn from are often those of women like you. Observing how women who share your background and experience face the changes of everyday life can be very helpful in learning to make equally smart decisions for yourself. In the following chapters, you will follow the lives of several women, much like you, with similar problems to solve. This book is an opportunity to look into the lives of other women in all kinds of situations and see the decisions they made after forty—and the results. The ways in which these women over forty use the *Ten Smartest Decisions* in their lives will help you understand how to cope with the new experiences of this stage of your life: how to create your future security, effectively manage changing roles, and maximize your personal satisfaction and enjoyment.

Eight Women's Stories

Julie, sixty-three, has worked full-time as a postal carrier since high school. She has been successful in her civil-service job, is fully vested in her retirement and has almost established her financial security. She loves to travel. Just as she is ready to retire, her parents are aging and having health problems. Her father is showing signs of dementia, and her mother cannot care for him anymore. Julie worries about them and wonders what she can do to help during this difficult time. Should she postpone her retirement plans and continue working? Or can she find daycare that will allow her to live the retirement she dreams of and to feel confident that her parents are okay? What decisions does she need to make to balance her personal life and the needs of the people she loves?

Karen, forty-six, is proud of her accomplishments. She raised two children as a single parent, and both are successful adults now. She has had a long, steady job as a grocery-store cashier, and now she's longing to do all the things she had to postpone for the benefit of her children. She worries that she's too old to date and find a relationship, and that she waited too long to try the singing career she has always wanted. Is there a chance that Karen can decide to make her dreams come true?

Laurie, forty-four, has worked hard to earn the medical degree she always wanted. She loves the opportunity to help people, to heal the sick and help her healthy patients remain strong. As an internist, she feels she sees the most interesting cases. But recently, she has lost her grandparents, then her mother, and several of her patients have had catastrophic illnesses and died. She experiences a lot of stress about the patients who are in pain, and those who have problems she cannot help. She is aware that her stress level is very high, and she sees signs of depression in herself. What decisions can Laurie make that will help her manage these painful aspects of life—her own grief and the despair of her terminally ill patients? What must she learn to be more helpful to these people she cares so much about?

Marian, fifty-four, a lawyer admitted to the bar in her state, used to work for a large law partnership, but went to work part-time after her daughter was born. She has been earning good money working as a temporary attorney, which gave her the flexible hours she needed to have as a single parent. How does she decide it's not too late to get her legal career back on track, become a partner in a good firm, or even to begin her own law practice?

Mary, fifty-one, has been a teacher since she graduated from college. She loves her work and has no intention of retiring early, but she would like to advance in her career. She could develop her management skills, with the goal of becoming a principal, or she could move into counseling and student services. Both positions require supplemental education, and Mary worries that if she doesn't make the right decision, she may wind up in a career path that is not as satisfying as her direct work with her students. How can she decide what will satisfy her in the future?

Rose, forty-two, trained to be a cosmetologist after high school and has been working as a hairdresser since that time. What she loves most about her work is talking with her clients and helping them with their problems. She dreams of being more effective at advising those in need and has decided to go back to school to obtain a license in alcoholism counseling. She doesn't know if she wants to work in a counseling center or if she wants to work for her-self. She worries that it's too late for her to go to college now, and it will take too long. She knows nothing about running a counseling business or starting a practice. How can Rose get her education and develop a good sense of what's involved in starting her own business?

Ruth, forty-one, has been married since high school and has two children, ages twenty-one and nineteen. Her husband, Paul, has been a successful businessman and is planning to retire in a few years. Ruth was a stay-at-home mom until her children were in grade school. For some extra income and stimulation, she then took a job in a women's-clothing store. Because Ruth wanted to be avail-able for her children after school, she couldn't devote the hours necessary for a management position, and her career development was limited. Now she has an opportunity to work full-time outside the home, but she and Paul soon could be traveling and enjoying his retirement. How does she decide what her priorities should be?

Sally, forty-five and divorced, has had a great career as a business executive, progressing steadily since she graduated with an M.B.A. Now her career has lost its excitement, she doesn't like the changes in her industry, and she feels frustrated and burnt-out. She wonders, "Is it too late for me to start a new career? What do I want to be when I grow up?"

Like you, these women have a lot of life experience, and though they have done well, all of them feel they have made mistakes. All of them have goals and dreams, and they all have questions about the future. They want to make changes in their lives, and they struggle with the changes occurring around them. The new stages of life they are facing require different decision-making skills than they have used before. We will follow their stories throughout the book and watch what happens as they face some of the most important decisions of their lives.

THIS BOOK IS ABOUT YOUR LIFE TODAY

Instead of the usual "women's topics" discussed in most self-help books for women, in this book you'll find eminently practical advice about the real issues of your life: your health, your finances, your family responsibilities, and your personal well-being and satisfaction.

The decisions presented here address every aspect of your life, and the skills taught can be used by anyone, at any age, to make smart decisions. What makes this a book for women after forty are the particular circumstances to which the decisions apply. As you read it, you'll realize that these are indeed the situations and the issues you face now or will confront in the next few years; and yet you will also find that its focus is broad enough to be helpful for many years to come.

You'll find yourself talking about the following decisions with other women your own age, with your family members, with the older women you know, and even with younger women who do not yet have your experience. The women's stories told throughout the book will echo the lives of yourself and your friends. In here you'll find answers to your questions and inspiration for new ideas. As you share these concepts with the women you know, you'll build support and a mutual network for implementing the decisions.

The journal you are asked to begin in the first exercise, and continue in subsequent processes throughout the book, will become a resource for evaluating new ideas, a record of your progress and growth, and a way to help you organize the changes you are making in your life. Because you're encouraged to do it in your own style, you'll find it becomes a valuable, lifelong tool and a pleasure to use.

This book is organized around the following ten decisions, which cover the most important issues virtually every woman, including you, will face in the years after forty. As you read this list, consider how they apply in your life now or how they will apply in the years to come.

THE TEN SMARTEST DECISIONS A WOMAN CAN MAKE AFTER FORTY

1. MAKE YOUR LIFE YOUR OWN. Decide to re-decide.

2. STEP INTO THE NEW YOU. Decide to change your life roles.

3. MAKE YOUR JOB A JOY. Decide to revitalize your career, or try a new one.

4. THE BUDDY SYSTEM. Decide to focus on friendship.

5. AN APPLE A DAY. Decide to stay healthy.

6. TAKE IT TO THE BANK. Decide to secure your financial position.

7. NEVER TOO LATE. Decide to be the person you might have been.

8. LIGHTEN UP. Decide to have more fun.

9. WHY ARE YOU HERE? Decide to create meaning in your life.

10. SHARE YOUR BOUNTY. Decide to give something back.

There are ten chapters, one for each of the *Ten Smartest Decisions.* In each chapter you'll find tools and information to help you make the wisest choices regarding these crucial aspects of your present and future life. Here you'll find out how to evaluate your choices in all these areas and how to make decisions you can trust are the right ones. You'll also find exercises and guidelines to help you with each decision and helpful illustrations from the stories of the women introduced previously.

Sharing the information here with friends and family members will help you open up topics that need discussion and cooperation. As you face all the changes, new opportunities, and new choices of this part of your life, the information here will help you feel more secure that you are considering all the necessary issues and making the smartest possible decisions.

You can read through the book for an overview, coming back to do the exercises as you need them; choose the chapters (decisions) that are most important to you right now; or read through the book systematically doing all the exercises and using the guidelines as you go along.

This book is offered in the spirit of sharing the experience that years of living, working, and counseling women have taught me. Life requires different decisions after forty, and often even a whole new perspective. Here's how to evaluate your life as it is and as you would like it to be. As you learn to make and implement these decisions, I know you will soon see the benefits and results of taking control of your life after forty.

Of course, you must decide which of the decisions apply to your life now. You will find a treasure of ideas and solutions here. It is my hope that this book will become a companion for the coming years, helping you to make smart decisions about each life circumstance as it arrives.

CHAPTER 1

Make Your Life Your Own: Decide to Re-decide

Full maturity . . . is achieved by realizing that you have choices to make.
—Angela Barren McBride

Women who realize that reaching forty is a new opportunity to reevaluate their lives and set new goals and priorities fare better than those who lament the passing of time or, worse yet, try to pretend it won't happen. You are reaching the point at which great changes occur: your children are growing up, you may be facing retirement, you realize you've achieved your major career goals, you experience the physical changes of maturity, your relationship focus changes, and you feel the need for a new philosophy of life. "If you're in your late thirties or early forties and feeling like you're in a prime time of life, you're not alone, "writes Tufts University researcher Miriam Nelson, Ph.D. in *Strong Women Stay Young.*" By our fourth decade most of us have our work lives under control and have also made time for joyful hobbies or meaningful volunteer work. If we had kids in our twenties, they've left the nest by now; if we had them in our early thirties they're beyond the can't-leave-them-alone-for-a-second toddler stage." Looking forward to the coming years and changes with anticipation and confidence will help you to surmount the difficulties and reap the rewards of a life well lived.

APPROACHING MIDLIFE—A NEW OPPORTUNITY

Although every woman faces a unique set of circumstances at midlife, all women experience changes, some of which are beyond their control. Children grow up, whether we try to hang on or not. Spouses also are going through changes, personally and in their careers. A spouse's retirement, for example, can have great impact on a couple's daily life. The death of a spouse, or a divorce, can leave you alone at a time when you were expecting to enjoy leisure time together. Menopause can bring changes in energy, sleep patterns, and temperament. Aging parents may present an extra burden at just the time your other responsibilities are easing. At forty, you may even decide it's time to begin the family you've previously been too busy to handle.

All of these new events can be difficult, and they require a careful response. The better your decisions about the changes are, the better the result you'll have and the easier they will be to survive. Children grow older and more independent and your time and energy are freed to follow dreams you never had time to pursue before. As children become adults, they can be more like friends and companions, giving back some of what they received from you in the past.

Exploring changes with your spouse can revitalize your relationship and strengthen your bond. If you have planned well, retirement can be a wonderful time, giving you the freedom to enjoy the most fun years of your life or providing a base from which to begin new enterprises. Becoming unexpectedly single, once you recover from the pain and loss, can mean being liberated from responsibilities and having the time to focus on the dreams you were never before free to pursue. Menopause, with the proper medical advice, can be the impetus to get yourself in shape and take care of your health, so you discover energy you never knew you had. The burden of elderly parents can be managed intelligently and lovingly—you may spark the healing of old rifts and discover a new warmth in your relationship. A decision to start a family late in life can be the impetus to reassess your finances, making sure you provide for the future of children who will be in college as you near seventy.

You can't simply opt out of some of these new life experiences. But you *can* choose how to respond to them. If you plan well and make smart decisions, weighing all the options and issues as the changes occur, you can create the most productive and satisfying years of your life, as well as an enjoyable future. But, like Ruth, you may feel overwhelmed and anxious when facing new situations.

Ruth's feelings are very mixed about the decisions that she sees in her future. She feels she has a good marriage, but she is quite frustrated and worried because her husband Paul has been planning retirement without considering what she wants to do. Ruth has not taken the time to sort through her options and decide what she wants in the upcoming years. As a result, she can't discuss their future plans thoroughly with him. If she doesn't resolve her own inner confusion and continues to be angry at him, she will set up a barrier between them, which will prevent them from thinking clearly and making plans that address both of their concerns. Eventually Ruth sees that not exploring her choices and discussing the possibilities with her husband would be a mistake.

Ruth is realizing that she doesn't have the tools she needs to make the decisions she faces. Change is difficult for most of us. You too may need to work through your own resistance and confusion when confronted with major life changes. You need to know what a smart decision is, and how to clear your thinking so you can use all the wisdom of your experience.

HOW TO MAKE SMART, MATURE DECISIONS

Smart decisions do not happen automatically. As I wrote in *The 10 Smartest Decisions a Woman Can Make Before 40,* there are five basic aspects to a smart decision. Because the elements of a good decision remain the same no matter how old you are, I am repeating them here. They are: self-awareness, research, appropriateness, support, and self-respect. As a mature woman the role of these aspects in your decision-making will be different than for a woman just starting out in life. Using your own experience, along with these principles, will ensure that each decision you make is a smart, considered, and effective one.

Even though you've made many decisions in your life, you may feel that you're not very comfortable with them. You may be used to making decisions at work, but feel less secure when they involve your family and friends. Or you may find that making decisions is quite simple when things are calm, but that you struggle when under stress or when things are hectic. Perhaps, in your experience, it is harder to make decisions when you know other people want to influence your choices. No matter what stumbling blocks you may encounter when faced with making decisions, knowing the components of a good decision can help you be sure you've examined all the necessary factors.

A traditional upbringing encourages women to develop their sensitive, nurturing sides. In spite of women's expanded roles in the workforce, we still receive mixed messages about the value of our strength and our intellect. It's no surprise that many women lack confidence about their ability to be objective and logical. But when you know that your decisions are founded on sound criteria, you can comfortably carry them out. And because your self-confidence will build with each success, you'll eventually spend more time making good decisions and less time wondering about whether you can.

Marian uses lots of critical-thinking skills as a lawyer, but when it comes to making decisions about her daughter and her parenting responsibilities, she has trouble being objective. "Sometimes I'm so full of guilt about wanting to move ahead in my practice. Mandy is now ten and doesn't need me around as much—she's always off to a friend's house or dance practice, so I could probably focus more on my career—and I'd really enjoy that. But a full-time career in law is demanding, and what if I wasn't here when she needed me? I'm in such turmoil, I can't even think clearly about it."

By considering the aspects of self-awareness, research, appropriateness, support, and self-respect, you'll gain the confidence you need to know your decisions are solid. As I noted earlier, the aspects of a smart decision are the same for women of all ages (and for men, for that matter), but they will apply differently to you in midlife than they did when you were younger.

Aspect 1: Self-awareness

As a mature woman, you know yourself in a lot of ways. You have seen who you are reflected in the eyes and in the responses of children, partners, family members, friends, and colleagues. You know how you react to stress, what you enjoy, and what you don't like. In your busy life, however, you don't always stop to consider yourself. Often when faced with a decision, you're so focused on the dynamics of the situation and on what everyone else wants or needs, you forget to ask, "What is my opinion? What do I need under these circumstances? What outcome is important to me?"

If that sounds selfish or self-centered, remember that you are only considering your own thoughts *along with* the wants, needs, and welfare of the others involved. If you don't understand what is important to *you*, however, you won't make the best possible decision.

Considering your own beliefs and feelings before you make a decision means they won't come back to haunt you later. No matter how important you feel a certain decision is to someone else, if you make a decision without self-awareness, you can find yourself harboring resentment and anger later on. If you feel coerced or pressured to make a decision that's uncomfortable for you, you won't find the motivation to carry it out.

Taking the time to examine your own thoughts and feelings, taking into consideration the kind of person you are, allows you to bring your truest self and all your experience to the decision-making process. Your feelings, ideas, and experience are part of what you need to know to make an accurate, effective decision that you can really carry out. Writing down your thoughts, feelings, and plans will help you clarify them.

Ruth writes in a journal to sort out her options and her feelings about Paul's retirement plans. Her years of job experience have taught her a lot about herself. She enjoys the responsibilities and rewards of working, she enjoys the camaraderie with her colleagues, and she also cares about her marriage. All these disparate feelings and wants are upsetting and confusing. "I love my husband, and I know how much he's looking forward to this. But I also love working. I didn't realize how hard it would be to face Paul's retirement. Is it wrong for me to want recognition and satisfaction of my own? Do I have to give up what I want because I love Paul? How do I resolve this dilemma? What can I do to make a decision that will honor both Paul and myself?"

If Ruth explores all her feelings, she'll be able to suggest some options to Paul, such as having a business of their own after his retirement, or encouraging him to use his free time in volunteer work that's meaningful to him while Ruth continues to work. Examining all your conflicting feelings may be a struggle, but the time to have the struggle is now, *before* you make your decisions.

AWARENESS THROUGH JOURNALING. One of the best ways to examine and sort out your feelings is to write them down in a notebook or journal (a practice many people know as "journaling"). One of the best things about writing is that it helps you put your life—

past, present, and future—into perspective. "The little trivial every-day junk that can weigh you down is all valuable raw material when you're writing. Your urge to strangle your health insurance company can be turned to good use . . . writing can help you figure out what's important to you and where you want to go next in your life," advises Susan K. Perry, Ph.D., a social psychologist and the bestselling author of *Writing in Flow: Keys to Enhanced Creativity:*

> Flow, that wonderful altered state of mind when time stops and whatever you're doing is the ONLY thing you want to be doing, can be experienced at ANY age. And in fact, the more you understand what it's like to lose yourself in some activity, the more easily you can do it. Writing is a great flow activity. When you write, you no longer feel the pressure of the clock. So it doesn't matter at all how old you are when you start. Dare to take the first step, which is to put pen to paper, or fingers to keyboard, and express yourself in words on paper.

Although **Marian** was able to support herself and her child by working part-time for several law firms, she felt she never had had a chance to fully develop her practice as an attorney. When she began to write in her journal, she discovered that now that her daughter was grown, she still had the longing to dedicate herself to a full-time legal career. Her experience as a mother had increased her interest in representing women in divorce and custody cases.

Colleagues at the law firm where she worked part-time told her she had great potential as a litigator, and she should go for it.

Friends and family also thought she'd do well. They told her she had given her daughter a very good foundation, and it was her turn to focus on her own goals. Professional colleagues said it might be a struggle, but they thought her legal skills and experience were strong enough for her to make it in a good law firm, or in her own practice. One colleague pointed out that working part-time had given her a more varied and wider experience than some attorneys who worked for a single firm. Some members of her family, however, advised Marian that her first loyalty was to her child, that it was too late to begin her career over again. By writing down her feelings, everyone's opinions, and her reactions to them, Marian discovered a lot more clarity about what she agreed with and what she didn't want.

"I was surprised at how effective it was for me to write everything down. In law school, we're taught to write out our arguments, make notes, and consider every angle of the case. When writing briefs we do the same thing. Keeping a journal was very similar. It helped me to organize my thoughts. I found myself writing what was actually a letter to myself. In considering others' advice, I wound up giving myself advice. Writing gave me a way to take a step back and look at my situation more objectively." Marian decided she was comfortable focusing a little less on being a mother and more on her law career. She decided to begin by applying to work in law firms with a well-developed family law practice, with the objective of eventually becoming a partner.

It is not unusual for a woman who writes out her thoughts to reach a conclusion similar to what others want for her. The difference is that after writing and analyzing your thoughts, you know that your solution is the right one for you. If you make your decision without the benefits of self-awareness, you may not feel certain that your decision is truly yours. And if people you respect or care for have voiced an opinion about the decision, consciously honoring your own perspective is all the more important.

Laurie has loved her career as an internist, and she's very proud of her expertise and her deep commitment to healing her patients. But recently her beloved mother died of cancer, many of her patients have passed away, and she has begun to wonder if medicine is truly the right field for her. Her friends and family became worried and urged her to reconsider her career. She found a psychotherapist to help her manage her feelings of being overwhelmed and depressed. The therapist aided Laurie in accepting her grief and in understanding that her hopeless feelings were connected with the loss of her mother.

"She helped me to see that in my mind, patients and others always came first. I never recognized my feelings and needs, or allowed myself to be important to me," explains Laurie. "Expressing my feelings in writing, as well as to the therapist, put them into perspective and made them seem less overwhelming. The grief gradually subsided. I also realized that my friends and family were worried about me, and that was the only reason they thought I should quit medicine. They thought it was too demanding and stressful for me, but in my therapy I realized that I really loved my work. It was the grief that was stressful." She was so relieved by working through her grief for her mother and her patients, she decided to move into hospice work, focusing on helping people at the end of life move through their transition more comfortably and get the most out of their last days. She feels confident in this decision, and now that her family and friends see how satisfied she is in her work, they are happy too.

Like these women, you can create a journal that will help you with all the exercises in every chapter of this book. Moreover, your journal can serve as a resource and a guide for your life to come.

Create a Life Journal

1. BEGIN A RECORD of your journey to your new life. You can use a blank book or notepad. Get a book or pad that seems to represent the life you want, with a cover that pleases you.

   Make sure the pages are big enough for you to write freely and that there's room to draw or paste in pictures if you want to. Use your journal for all the exercises in this and the following chapters to create a record of your new decisions.

Karen, who wants to sing, uses a large blank book with old sheet music pictured on the cover. **Julie,** who gardens (in the little spare time she has) because the new growth of her flowers gives her hope, chose a large pad with sunflowers on the cover. **Ruth** was delighted to find a big scrapbook with images of foreign money, representing to her the desire for travel and a career.

2. CREATE A TITLE PAGE. You can use your sense of humor: "What I Want to Be When I Grow Up." Take a phrase from a favorite poem or book: "What I Might Have Been." Or, like **Rose,** just name it after yourself—"Rose's Journal." Use fancy lettering, by hand or on your computer, draw (or cut and paste) pictures or

your own designs on your title page. Make it as beautiful, joyous, funny, formal, or dramatic as you wish.

3. BEGIN WRITING. The exercises in this and other chapters are all designed to be written in your journal, but I strongly encourage you to use your journal for other purposes outside the confines of this book. Your journal is a dialogue with yourself. You can write yourself letters, record memories, add photos, and draw pictures. Quotations, poetry, Bible verses, or song lyrics can help express your mood and feelings. Make it the workbook for creating the life you want.

Profound events, such as the death of someone close to you, an illness, or a family drug problem or other crisis, can make it very difficult to understand your own feelings about decisions that you need to make.

Laurie, normally in charge and competent, was so overwhelmed by the depth of her grief that she lost her ability to know what she wanted or to think clearly. The power of her feelings made her distrust her own life experience and career history. The expert help of her therapist and the writing she was asked to do enabled her to work through her feelings and even use them effectively to enhance her next career decision.

No matter how difficult the problem, taking the time to write it out will help you to know what you think and feel, and in turn will help to guide you to a smart decision.

FLEXIBILITY. As you well know from your own experience, life doesn't always go as planned. For those times, knowing yourself can help you be flexible and adaptable. If you have thoroughly examined your ideas and feelings in advance, you'll have enough information to make a new decision when your original idea doesn't pan out.

Mary loves her teaching career, and she feels successful. In her current position, however, there is little potential for economic growth, and her retirement benefits are limited. If she continues her education and moves in to administrative work, she can become a principal; or, if she takes psychology, she can become a school counselor. Financially these are both good decisions, but Mary is not certain she will like either job as much as she likes teaching. There are also many unknowns about how successful she could be as a principal or a counselor. Both are high-pressure jobs. "I felt caught between two unknowns. Staying where I was would be the easiest thing, but it also made my future retirement very uncertain. But it was difficult to choose a new career path without much information about what it would be like," she remembers. "Being a principal or a counselor might be so stressful that it would take all the joy out of work for me. I love working with children and inspiring them to learn and grow, so that is not easy to give up. I just don't know if I'd like another job as well, and I don't think the extra money would be enough if I didn't like the work."

Mary decided to take some of the classes required for each position—using some alternative methods such as classes online and weekends so she could keep teaching. The coursework would be valuable to her in her teaching and also give her a better idea of what the more-lucrative jobs entailed. She also decided to talk to the principal of her school and other people she has met over the years to get more information about her alternatives. Taking classes would not interfere with the work she loves now, and would provide a solid base for changes in the future. Mary's awareness of her concerns motivated her to take the time and effort to try out her new options before making her final decision. She was flexible enough to want to try things out before she committed a lot of time and money.

Sometimes life presents surprises—and you grow out of situations that were fine a few years ago, as **Sally** did: "After twenty years I've really gone about as far as I can go in this business, and I'm surprised to find myself bored. Corporate finances are just not as interesting to me as they were when I was younger. Then there was always something new to learn. Now I feel as though I've seen everything. I need a new challenge, something different. I'm tired of coming in to an office every day, tired of the same old reports and routines. I've been reading some books and magazines about being an entrepreneur, and it sounds intriguing. I want more control over my time and my life. I know it's not easy, but I'd like to find out what it would take to begin my own business."

Stepping back a bit and looking at her situation more objectively, Sally can see that she has talents and skills she can draw on, and that the business culture has changed with the advent of the Internet. Sally is beginning to think she can begin her own business as a consultant. Using the very expertise that causes her to feel unchallenged now, she can create excitement for herself by helping businesses be more financially effective and efficient. Researching what is necessary to be successful as a consultant and the challenge of designing a Web site for her new business has her excited and energized again.

As you gain self-awareness, you can also use what you know about yourself to make difficult or disappointing situations more manageable. **Julie** is coming to realize that she can't successfully juggle all of her responsibilities, and that perhaps she needs to get some help.

Julie is very grateful for her civil-service job with the U.S. Postal Service. The work has been rewarding and the job security and excellent benefits have allowed her to create financial security for herself. She was looking forward to traveling on her vacations and retiring in a few years, but she is beginning to realize that her parents, who were always self-sufficient, are going to need more care than she thought. "I love my mom and dad, and it's so hard to see them struggling," Julie laments. "I've always been able to do what I wanted to do with my free time, but now I spend it looking after my parents. Dad is getting so forgetful, and sometimes he's irritable and angry for no reason. Mom just can't handle him. He leaves the gas burners on in the kitchen, forgets to lock the door, and we had to take his car keys away because he's become dangerous on the road. I thought I could help them by myself, but I'm realizing that their problems are too much for me. I'm getting burned out and even making bad decisions. I guess it's time to admit that I need some help, and to get it I suppose I have to give up some of the control."

Like these women, you can use what you learn about yourself to make your decisions more effective and appropriate to your personality, to adapt to changes, to make the most of your strengths, and to help compensate for your weaknesses. This expanded awareness of your needs, and the circumstances, will give you the flexibility you need to negotiate new situations.

Aspect 2: Research

Most decisions require some sort of research, even if it is only to clarify the problem you need to solve. When I help a client to understand her problem clearly, to research all the necessary facts and circumstances, and to explore possible options and outcomes, she finds it much easier to make a good decision. Often, we try to make decisions on incomplete information, hearsay, or guesswork—and in the process, feel insecure about whether we've decided well.

If you feel insecure about making a decision, trust your insecurity. It means you're not prepared to decide, most likely because you don't feel you understand or know enough about the decision's ramifications.

Ruth feels very insecure about the future because she doesn't know how Paul's retirement will affect their plans. Paul has been looking forward to this time for so long, he just assumes she's as excited about it as he is. Neither of them has all the facts about how the other one feels, and neither understands what all the options are. When Ruth begins to ask some questions about Paul's plans, and shares her own desires, the facts will begin to come to light. When she asks retired friends whether they are enjoying this stage of life, she will gain even more information and perspective. Ruth's thoughts will become increasingly clear as she learns about retirement.

Focusing on past mistakes or previous decisions that didn't have a favorable result can also make you hesitate in making important decisions now. Research will help you see what, if anything, you could have done differently in the past or that the current situation bears no resemblance to your past experience.

Mary loves teaching but worries that it won't provide sufficient income for her to retire comfortably. She feels too worried to think clearly about making a career move into administration or counseling. She remembers that she was miserable in her first teaching job, and because of that experience, she's afraid to leave this job she likes. "I made the wrong choice once, and I could do it again," she worries. "How can I know whether counseling or administrative work would be satisfying?"

Mary decides to spend a year exploring the career possibilities of counseling or administration before making a decision. She'll talk to friends who have similar jobs and take some days off to sit in with counselors and principals, so she can see what the jobs are really like.

RESEARCH OPTIONS. There are a number of effective ways to research the facts and your options. **Ruth** used one of them when she asked Paul and her friends for their ideas and experience—she learned from the experience of others. In the following example, **Sally** researches the facts and also devises an experiment where she can learn from experience.

During her career, Sally often had the chance to advise other companies on business practices; she was well respected in her field and she enjoyed her work. But when she began to think about striking out into business for herself, she was not sure that consulting full-time would be as rewarding as these occasional experiences. As a "test," she decided to try a consulting job that was a little more extensive. She did a lot of research and thoroughly checked out the company that wanted help—and also the rules of her own company, to make sure there would be no conflict of interest. Working with this one company would be a trial situation in which she would get to see what consulting was like, to "try out" her expertise in this new arena, and to explore how it felt to be a consultant rather than an employee.

What Sally learned during this experience convinced her that her own consulting service could be successful. "This more extensive consulting job was exciting, and as I gained experience, I became more confident that I could do it," she says with a smile. "That consulting job provided a great 'trial run' for me. I got firsthand experience that convinced me that my business knowledge was sufficient, and I would be able to create enough opportunities to succeed financially. As long as I didn't work for my company's competition or divulge its private information, my employer didn't object. My supervisor even encouraged me to take a few small consulting jobs with suppliers, which enhanced the relationship between the companies. That was a great beginning for me. Before long, I was getting known as an effective consultant, and the requests began to come in. I was self-employed almost before I realized it, and all because I decided to research what it would be like."

Any new venture requires research. If it's a new business, you have to find information about the markets, the potential problems, the competition, and the day-to-day operating issues and costs. If it's a new hobby or activity, you need to find out what equipment is needed and perhaps take some classes to get started. If it's a new life experience, such as getting married, having a baby, or facing retirement, you need good factual information to be prepared for the many changes that are part of the situation. Sometimes this takes time, which is difficult to accept, because we are usually eager to make the decision right away.

In *The 10 Smartest Decisions a Woman Can Make Before 40,* I wrote: "The major components of research are (1) your own experience; (2) the experience of others you know; and (3) the available information. Using all three of these components means you will have enough information to make an informed decision." As you can see, these components are the same for women over forty. A smart decision is always a smart decision.

YOUR EXPERIENCE. After forty, you have a lot of experience of your own which, if you know how to use it, can serve as a highly useful data bank. Search your own past for related experiences. You can see how you reacted to certain conditions, such as stress or unknown outcomes, or explore past relationships to see if you encountered a similar situation to the one you are facing now. Although this may seem obvious, or even automatic, if you don't consciously take the time to think about related past experiences, you may not benefit from what you did before. Sometimes this kind of research involves learning from past mistakes, and sometimes it involves applying familiar information in a slightly different way.

Mary and **Sally** both used their past work experience to find resources for the new things they wanted to try. Mary was cautious about her current ambitions because she had learned from the previous teaching position she hadn't enjoyed.

The Wheel-Chart Technique

You can use your journal to explore what you already know about your present situation from your past experience. One helpful exercise is to make a "wheel chart"—that is, write a one- or two-word description of the decision you need to make on a blank page. Mary and Sally could both write "career change," or be more specific with "counseling" for Mary and "consulting" for Sally. Circle that word, and then draw spokes out from it. At each spoke, write one of the things you know about your experience that relates to the central idea. For example, Mary could write "helps children," "need more school," "better salary," "better retirement," "Can I do it?"—all radiating out from the central word. When you have written down all the thoughts and related experiences, ideas for what to do next, and the like around the central idea, often you'll realize that you already know a lot more than you thought about the central topic. This technique will also give you ideas about further information you need and resources where you can obtain it.

TAP INTO YOUR NETWORK. Learning from others' experience is a byproduct of networking. Regardless of your plan, whether it's to become a foster parent, change careers, or get married, discussing your situation with those who have experience will help you make better decisions.

Change is always unsettling. When you're doing something familiar, you feel a sense of control. With a new situation, you're not sure what the future will bring. (Although who ever really knows their future?) Many women (and men) feel insecure about their ability to adapt to the new experience.

Mary worries that changing from the career she loves (although she'll be in a closely related field) will spoil her joy in her profession.

To diminish her uncertainty, she begins to learn from the experiences of others. She arranges to spend time with them in their work. In this way some aspects of their experiences become part of her own experience.

Guidelines for Learning from Others' Experiences

Here are some of the guidelines for learning from others, adapted from those I included in *The 10 Smartest Decisions a Woman Can Make Before 40*. For many years I have taught these guidelines to clients, students, and workshop attendees of every age, because so many people need to know how to research new decisions before they make them. No matter what you want to learn about, you can find it out in these ways:

- Ask people you know who are experienced or who can introduce you to someone who is.

- Attend a class or a lecture by an expert in the field and have some questions ready to ask if you get an opportunity.

- Read a related biography or first-person account.

- Find a related Web site on the Internet and ask your questions there.

- Call a college or business and ask to speak to a faculty member who is an expert in that topic.

- Go to a meeting of a group or an organization focused on that field.

- Search the records of your local newspaper for a related story and contact the reporter or the people mentioned in the story.

GET THE FACTS. People are a great resource, but don't forget there are plenty of other ways to do research. Books, newspapers, magazines, and the Internet are treasure troves of information about almost everything under the sun, from travel to medical issues, to proper etiquette for unusual situations. (What fork do you use if you're invited to dinner at the White House?)

One book, magazine article, or Web site will often lead you to others. And don't overlook the knowledge of the librarian at your favorite public or college library. He or she can lead you to a wealth of resources, in person or over the phone.

Aspect 3: Appropriateness

Although self-awareness and research are important, your decision won't be a smart one unless it takes into account factors outside yourself. Is this decision going to work in your real life? Will it upset the people around you? (That doesn't automatically make it a bad decision.) Is it financially sound? Is it realistic? Can you follow through on it? All of these questions are related to the appropriateness of your decision. The better your understanding of these factors, the more effective your decision will be.

Ruth is frustrated because she doesn't feel considered in Paul's retirement plans. Nonetheless she realizes that they are and have been a good team, they love each other, and they've worked through many difficulties in the course of their marriage. She knows that it would be very inappropriate to make unilateral decisions at this point. She must take Paul's plans and feelings into consideration. She also realizes that he is not deliberately ignoring her wants—he's just enthused and assuming she shares his feelings. "I realize that I haven't been clear enough with Paul about wanting to continue working when he retires," she says with a furrowed brow. "Paul thought I'd be as excited about his travel plans as he was. I need to find out more about what he's thinking and make sure he understands how I feel. Perhaps we'll need a counselor to help us talk about this, but I know I'm not going to make a rash decision that will create a problem in our marriage. No decision is worth the loss of this great relationship. When I find a way to discuss this more clearly with him, we'll probably be able to make some mutual arrangement that will work."

In the following chapters, I will discuss many aspects of appropriate decisions. When you look ahead to the potential results of your decision *for yourself,* as well as the impact of the changes you're making on the people around you, you will get the best possible outcome. To be appropriate, you must coordinate your new decision with the major components of your life. Deciding to make big changes, even if they disrupt the lives of others (for example, if you decide to move or change your schedule), can be beneficial—but you need to know the most likely outcome in advance and prepare yourself and those around you.

Aspect 4: Support

New decisions, especially the major ones, are usually accompanied by some insecurity and anxiety in yourself, and perhaps in the people around you. If you're learning new things, you'll have the added insecurity of feeling incompetent until you've attained the necessary skills and information. For women over forty, this "beginner" feeling can be very uncomfortable. You've lived long enough to feel skilled at most of the things you do, and the awkwardness and uncertainty of a new situation are often hard to bear.

For encouragement and assistance during this transitional stage, it's necessary to find support. If you're making a small decision, the support of friends and family (and yourself) is probably sufficient. But if you're making significant new choices that involve changing behaviors, learning new things, or confronting a difficult situation, professional support may be valuable. For example, if you're making a behavioral change to improve your health, the support of your doctor, a knowledgeable guide (such as a personal trainer, sponsor, therapist, teacher, or dietician), and/or a class (aerobics, yoga, twelve-step group, or weight-loss group) can help you stay motivated. With experts and/or colleagues, you'll have a chance to share useful information and similar experiences. You may even have the benefit of an individual who helps you monitor your progress. Having such support will help you carry out your decision, even if it involves demanding challenges.

Rose knows how helpful group support and good information sources are when making difficult changes. She has seen many of her salon clients and family members improve their lives with the help of Alcoholics Anonymous and other support groups. She wants to help more effectively than she can by just listening and being sympathetic to her beauty clients. She also wants to improve her earning power. She is smart enough to recognize that she, too, will need support. Rose has attended Al-Anon meetings for several years and knows some good sponsors and counselors. She also is very involved in her church, so she decides to talk to the pastor about resources for education. She identifies the family members who will help and support her dream and tells them she wants their encouragement and advice during the transition process. She asks her church prayer group to pray for her success and finds that they are interested in her progress. As she shares her plan with others who are already licensed counselors, she discovers that she can get her education more efficiently and quickly than she could have when she was eighteen. There are college programs for working adults, and she can take courses on the Internet that will give college credit toward her degree. All the people she is asking to support her goals now will later be resources for client referrals.

Marian is anxious about making the change from working for a legal registry to working full-time for a law firm. She has begun to let the other lawyers she works with know she's ready to move into full-time legal work and to get on a partnership track. The lawyers she works for know the quality of her work and several of them have encouraged her to apply for a job with their firms. She has also kept a list of lawyers she has worked with on other temporary assignments, and she has updated her résumé, written some personal cover letters to these people, and begun her job search. She has also found an employment counselor at the lawyers' registry who knows of her interests, her good reputation, and her exemplary history with the agency. The counselor has begun looking for a suitable full-time job for her, and her friends have helped her decide which law firms to apply to. Her professional group, the Association of Women Trial Attorneys, also provides a job clearinghouse, and she has notified the committee members that she's looking. The support she gets now will help her find a good position, and after she's hired, she can rely on this support system when she needs information or encouragement.

Laurie got a lot of help in working through her grief for her mother from her therapist and her grief therapy group. Much to her surprise, when she decided to move to hospice work, the same people supported her decision. They told her how comforting she had been to the other people who were grieving and validated her belief that she would be effective at working with patients in hospice.

Aspect 5: Self-respect

Self-respect is the final element of a good decision. Self-respect differs from self-awareness: the latter is a good *understanding* of your thoughts and personality traits; self-respect, on the other hand, is a good *regard* for yourself as a human being. If you are to have the commitment, enthusiasm, and energy to carry out the decisions you make, your choices must be an expression of your personal rights. You have a right to be well treated, to create a satisfying life for yourself, to value your own intelligence and creativity. You deserve to have good friends and good family relationships, as well as a good relationship with yourself. The decisions you make should reflect these rights. Sacrificing yourself to please others leads to bad decisions. If you lack self-respect, you're likely to make decisions that result in your being cheated or disappointed. When you value yourself, you'll make smart decisions that will lead to better results for you.

Laurie gained self-respect when she acknowledged the depth of her grief and the effect it was having on her. With her renewed confidence she was able to end her depression, make an important career move, and obtain more satisfaction from her work. Now she feels that she is doing very important work to ease her patients' emotional pain as well as their physical ailments.

Marian earned her self-respect through caring for herself and her daughter. She's confident enough to take some personal risks and try to make her dreams come true. Her own life experience as a single mom, her ability to complete law school and work for the registry, and the difficulties she has overcome form the basis of her confidence in herself.

In action, self-respect means making your own decisions in your own way—compromising neither your needs nor your integrity in the process. If you wait too long in making a decision, you'll lose the opportunity and the decision will be made without you. For example, if you waver long enough about making a decision, the deadline can pass, or someone else can decide without your input. Making decisions with your self-respect in mind means you'll make decisions according to your own values, even while you're considering the impact on others.

REACTING, RESPONDING, AND INITIATING

Of course, you need to consider factors other than your own wants and needs when you make decisions. Our decisions affect, and are affected by, other people, circumstances, and unforeseeable events. Reacting and responding are the two basic options you have when you make a decision in response to another person, circumstance, or event. When you initiate, you decide to take action on your own;

although another person or event may be related to your decision, the external factor is not the primary cause of your behavior.

Reacting

A reaction is something you say or do in the moment, often before your brain is fully engaged. You don't take the time to think the action through—you just do it. This is a great resource to have in emergencies. When you react, you: save someone from danger (for example, yank a friend back if she starts to walk in front of a moving car); instantly comfort a family member or friend who has experienced a loss, without even knowing the details of what has happened; grab a smoldering potholder that's too close to the stove; swerve the car to avoid a child who runs out into the street.

Your ability to do this is a small miracle, gained through eons of evolution. Those who were capable of instant reactions (fight or flight) survived to pass the ability down to us, however, reacting to an event before you think can also create problems. You can react emotionally without considering factors that might change the way you see the situation or make a snap judgment that later turns out to be wrong. Although your ability to react quickly can be very valuable, by itself it will not suit most situations.

Responding

When you consider someone else's wants and needs, know enough facts about the situation, and then consciously choose what to do, you're responding rather than reacting. Responding takes a little more time and thought than reacting, and the behavior is under greater control. You respond many times a day. If your mate comes home tired and irritable, and you speak a little more softly, or allow a little extra time for unwinding, you're responding with love and thoughtfulness. If your child has a big game or performance, and you and the rest of your family show up and cheer him on, you're responding with encouragement and support. If your financial situation gets tight, and you take an extra job or work overtime to make ends meet, you're responding with extra effort. If you hear a traffic jam reported on the radio, and you take a different route, you're responding with a smart, safe alternative. A decision based on an intelligent response can solve problems, smooth over difficult situations, get you out of tough corners, and enhance all your relationships.

But response and reaction are not enough. Women seem to excel at both, perhaps because we've been encouraged and rewarded for doing so. Responding and reacting are the behaviors traditionally expected from women, as they are inextricably connected with the needs or wants of others. It's much more difficult for many women to initiate actions on their own, without an outside stimulus to respond to.

Initiating

Decisions you initiate on your own, for your own reasons, become increasingly necessary as you age and as you experience life changes. In the next chapters, we will consider many of the types of decisions you will need to initiate, including changing roles, financial security, and creating meaning and richness in your life.

To initiate actions from scratch requires forethought and a plan. First, you have to know what you want to accomplish, either in the short term, the long term, or both, and then create a plan to do it. The following exercise will help you formulate your plan.

The Wish List

1. WISHES AND DREAMS. Think back on your life, from your childhood until the present. In your journal, make a list of all the things you feel you might have missed. Is there anything you have always wanted to do? Anything you dreamed of? Anything you've seen someone else do that you envy? If you could do anything you ever wanted to do, without considering anyone else or financial constraints, what would that be? What would you do if you won the lottery? Write your wishes and dreams in your journal. Perhaps you always wanted to take gymnastics or ballet, sing, write, act, or be an artist, but were too shy or felt you didn't have enough talent. Perhaps you wanted to go to college or take different subjects in school. What do you wish you had learned? Perhaps you wanted children and didn't have them, or didn't want the children you had. Perhaps you wanted to travel, try out for the Olympics, have your own business, or join the Armed Forces or the Peace Corps. Maybe you wanted a more exciting career or to be a stay-at-home mom.

2. UPDATE THE WISHES. Now review what you've written and update it to today. How would it feel if you decided to try it now? It's never too late to try. Even if you never were athletic, and your dream was to be a gymnast or a ballet dancer, there

are classes and instruction for adults who are just beginning. You can still learn anything you wanted to learn, or try, in some form—whatever you missed. Even if you can't be the mother you wanted to be, you can be a foster parent or a hospital or school volunteer. It's not too late to get your education or to try a new career. Write down what your fantasy would look like if you tried it today: "Maybe I can't be a tap-dancer in the movies, but today I can take a tap-dancing class for fun and exercise." "Perhaps it's not too late to go to law school—I could take start classes in the fall and even begin a career." "I'm too old for the military, but I can get into good physical shape—I can hike, camp, and play sports." "I could still take classes in religion, even though I may not want to become a minister."

3. RESEARCH. Look in your area for opportunities. Using your updated wishes, find related local activities, classes, or clubs. You can research on the Internet, among friends, at the library, in local college catalogs, city parks and recreation departments, and volunteer organizations. Write down the possibilities that you find.

4. MAKE A PLAN. Write down a plan to begin to bring your wish into reality. If you want to take a class, find out when it begins and register. If you want to try a sport or other activity, find out how to get involved. Begin with the smallest step you can take to realize your dream and plan a series of steps to accomplish what you want to do. Plan to include some people you can count on to be supportive of your dream.

Karen knows the value of planning. Because she has worked her way up to supervisor of all the cashiers, she organizes all of their schedules. As a working mom she had to learn to be very organized at home as well, but she never got her personal life in order. Whatever she wanted to do always seemed to come last on the list, and usually she never got to it at all; in her mind, doing things for her own enjoyment and well-being was "selfish" and "not important." Now that she is financially secure and her children are nearly grown, she is finding she has more leisure time, and she's beginning to think about what she wants. "I always wanted to be a singer, and I have sung in church and for my friends, but now that I have some time and a little extra money, I want to study voice and see what I can do with it." She found a vocal-performance class at the adult-outreach department of a local college and made a plan to enroll. "For the first time, I'm planning something that's entirely for me and about me, and not because of anyone else. It makes me feel important to myself, and as if my life has some personal meaning after all. I love my kids, but I'm glad they don't need me as much as they once did. I've been last on my own to-do list for way too long."

RE-DECIDING THE RIGHT WAY

When you use the five aspects of a smart decision, you'll have the confidence of knowing you've made the best decision you can under your present circumstances. As you gain an awareness of your own needs through writing and reflection, research all the pertinent facts from your own and others' experience, make sure your choices are appropriate to your situation and surroundings, create and use support systems, and acknowledge your right to integrity, you'll find that making decisions becomes easier. These tools can be applied to any problem, and each time you use them, your decision will be easier to carry out because you'll feel secure that it is reasonable, balanced, effective, and correct.

The following chapter, "Step Into the New You: Decide to Change Your Life Roles," contains exercises that will help you use these decision-making techniques to reinvent yourself and create the life you want.

CHAPTER 2

Step Into the New You: Decide to Change Your Life Roles

> *A woman's life can be a succession of lives, each revolving around some emotionally compelling situation or challenge, and each marked off by some intense experience.*
>
> —Wallis Simpson, Duchess of Windsor

At this stage of your life, you may be surprised to find yourself letting go of old roles. Voluntarily or not, you will find familiar situations altering and evolving. The passage of time changes your circumstances, both positively (you feel more confident in your experience, you may be more financially secure, you enjoy watching your children succeed as teenagers and young adults) and negatively (you miss your role as "Mom," you get bored with your work, you worry about aging).

THE NEW YOU

Whether you initiate role changes yourself or find yourself faced with alternatives you didn't choose, making conscious decisions about the roles you take on will create more satisfaction and pleasure in life.

Ruth's children are growing up. Her daughter Susan, at twenty-one, has a job, a husband, and an apartment of her own. Ruth's son, Jason, is nineteen and in his freshman year at college. Both are gone most of the time and need very little advice from Ruth. Her role as "Mom" is largely honorary these days. "I know how the Queen Mother must feel," she says. "All my hard-won parenting expertise seems pretty useless these days, and I feel lost rattling around this empty house."

Until Ruth takes an active part in deciding what she wants her life to be about when her parental role is over, she will continue to feel useless. Even if her children marry and produce grandchildren Ruth can fuss over and indulge, she will probably never be a full-time parent again.

This can be a great opportunity for Ruth to re-create her life, to do things she has always wanted to do and never had the time for, or to try something completely new and different. Ruth has some research to do—searching inside herself to discover unfulfilled dreams and searching for information and new options. She has the chance to revitalize her marriage, which has settled into a comfortable but somewhat predictable routine. She can choose to find an outlet for her energy and wisdom through education, a career, or through charitable work.

Women who have had satisfying and stimulating careers often find that work is less rewarding than it used to be and long for a new challenge or more freedom.

Sally, forty-five, has extensive experience and expertise as a business executive. She doesn't have the enthusiasm for it that she used to, and her role as the Wonder Woman executive is wearing thin.

"I spent more than twenty years conquering new horizons, making great deals, and being excited by the challenges of my career. Lately it all seems boring, and there's nothing new. I don't want to begin a whole new career, but I need a change."

Sally's options include creating more time for travel and leisure, changing to another field to create more challenge, or even reanalyzing her finances and considering an early retirement. If she takes charge and makes smart choices now, she still has plenty of time to make the changes she wants.

On the other hand, **Mary** loves her teaching career. She has no intention of retiring early, but she needs a new challenge. Administrators in her school district are encouraging her to move into a vice-principal position, with the goal of becoming a principal, and she also has an opportunity to move into counseling and student services. No matter which path she takes, she will need further education. "The prospect of going back to graduate school is exciting and frightening. It's been a long time since I was the student, but what if I make the wrong choice and wind up unhappy? What if being a principal or a counselor is not as satisfying as working with students? Which one would be the right choice?"

Mary recognizes that she needs a change, but worries about making the wrong choices. What can she do to make sure this critical period of her life brings smart decisions and great results?

The maturity of midlife brings new insights, opportunities, and altered circumstances. Forty years of life experience make a profound difference in your abilities, philosophy, and wisdom. As a result of this experience, you may find, as many women do, that what was a smart decision for you in your twenties no longer meets your needs. As you create new roles for yourself, you'll find that you feel more grounded, more self-aware and ready for a new challenge. This is an exciting time, because the new you is in charge of who you are and what you do.

The extreme focus on youth by the media may make it seem that getting older is a downward slide, but it doesn't have to be. We are so long-lived now, compared to our ancestors, that our productive years can easily last until seventy-five or eighty, and, if we carefully plan for a secure retirement, we can experience a creative blossoming, or a "second middle age" as it has been called.

Hunter College researcher Lydia Bronte, Ph.D., director of the Long Careers Study, interviewed 150 high achievers between the ages of sixty-five and 101. Her study found that by age fifty, these exceptional people had a strong understanding of who they were and what they wanted to accomplish. After they had completed life tasks such as building professional networks and raising their families, they experienced a surge of creative energy. They wisely used this midlife "second wind" to achieve amazing new things. By being sure you make smart decisions now, you too can have a vital, satisfying, creative, and even astonishing life after forty.

Endless Possibilities

Change is frightening, yes, but it can also be exciting. No matter what pressure you're under, what tough decisions you face, keep in mind that you can turn this chaos into a new beginning, a new freedom to choose. Rather than feeling that you must take life as it's handed to you, you can now approach it as a buffet of options. When you are faced with the loss of an old role, or become bored with familiar tasks, use that impetus to try something new and exciting.

Have you always wanted to write? "Starting to pursue a writing dream a little later in life can actually be a plus," explains Dr. Perry, author of *Writing in Flow:*

> All the experiences you've saved up may give you a much better ability to see patterns, and that can help you write a more powerful story, essay, article, or book. Many highly successful writers didn't begin pursuing writing until they were past the first flush of youth. But once they discovered how rewarding it can be—emotionally, and sometimes even in terms of fame and fortune—they wouldn't give up writing for anything.

A good example is Julie Andrews. In her sixties, the actress/singer is now a successful author of children's books.

Do you want to act? Have your own business? Dance or make music? Read all the great books? Study religion or philosophy? Run a marathon or practice yoga? Design fashions, create computer art, take up photography or throw pottery? Play a sport? Buy or build your own house, or remodel the one you have? Travel? Become physically fit? Learn to invest in the stock market? Begin meditating? Here is your chance. Whether your new decision involves making money or using free time, whether your desire is intellectual, artistic, spiritual, or physical, you can begin now to make it a reality in your life.

Sally, after creating more time for herself by working at home, is pursuing her dream of travel. She found both housing exchanges abroad and opportunities to teach English on the Internet. She's traveling more than she ever thought possible and earning money, too.

Until this point in your life, you may have been so concerned with your daily responsibilities you didn't think much about your future. But as children grow up and need you less, as you witness family members aging, as you feel more secure in your abilities, you'll find the future beckons (either threateningly or invitingly) before you. At an age that used to be considered old, you can reasonably expect decades of active life.

Unfortunately, there is no guarantee that your future will be joyful. You probably have seen women shut themselves away from the world as they get older, fading into an aimless, sad, lonely old age. You may have seen women you know put everything they could into raising their families, only to have grown children move away and leave them on their own. You may also have seen vibrant older women "blossom" into self-assured, active, and happy individuals with purpose and energy. What kind of old age are you planning?

Helping her elderly parents has given **Julie** a new perspective on her own life. The problems of old age are right in front of her eyes, and she realizes that her parents' current difficulties could be her own in a decade or two. Because she is single, with no children, she will be responsible for arranging her own care, so while she's looking for help with her parents, she's also thinking of her own future. She wants to find a living situation that will guarantee care and also permit her to do more of the things she loves to do. For the first time, Julie and her mother are planning to take a much-needed vacation, a cruise for just the two of them, to rest and relax. Because gardening is her favorite pastime, Julie has also decided to take some courses in gardening and join a gardening club. She wants to make connections with others who enjoy horticulture and perhaps find a friend who will travel with her to visit the world's great gardens.

You can explore new and different roles and opportunities with the following exercise.

New Life Evaluation

In this exercise, you'll use your journal to explore all your roles, past, present, and future.

1. LIST YOUR ROLES. Write down all the roles you are accustomed to playing in your life until now. Begin with the broadest categories, such as "wife," "mother," "executive," "assistant," "daughter," "sister," and "friend." Then break each big category down into smaller roles. **Ruth** divided her "mother" role into "cook," "caretaker," "chauffeur," "nurturer," "confidante," "dresser," "shopper," "nurse," "keeper of the budget," "maid," "disciplinarian," and several others. Take enough time to make a full list—you may want to do this over a few days, as you observe yourself playing your many roles. Add some fun roles like "sex goddess," "queen of the world," and "comedienne."

2. EDIT YOUR LIST. Take some crayons, markers, or colored pens and pencils and *mark all over your list.* Cross out the roles you really dislike, underline or circle the ones you love, then comment on all of them (funny, nasty, silly, or sensible comments are all fine). This is a chance to begin to take charge of those roles, possibly for the first time. Notice what you feel as you do this. If you're having a great time and laughing, then you're well

on your way to letting go of these old roles. If you feel like shutting the book and running away, you may be afraid of what you'll learn here. Be patient with yourself, and remember that you can create whatever you want in your life—it's not too late. If you feel rebellious, that's a good sign—the energy you will need to make changes is being generated in your emotion. If you feel angry, you can use that energy to create change also. If you feel sad or overwhelmed, allow those feelings to surface and pay attention to them. Within these feelings are the secrets you need to know to create the new life you really want.

Julie, facing the problems of her elderly parents, has very mixed feelings. In her role as a daughter, she is grief-stricken. As "parent" taking care of her own parents, she feels responsible, nurturing, and stressed. As a single woman who is feeling she can finally enjoy some free time, she's resentful and disappointed.

3. ADD NEW RULES. After you've commented all you want on your accustomed roles, consider some new ones. Look in your journal at your "wish list" of things you always wanted to do someday. What did you want to be when you grew up? Is there anything you regret doing, or not doing? What sounds like fun? What sounds like the "real you"? What have you been envious of that other women (or men) have or do? What improbable things that people do in novels, movies, or on TV shows appeal to you? What would you do if you won the lottery? Don't be practical with this list—you've been practical your whole life. This is the time to be creative, fanciful, and imaginative. If your fairy

godmother, a genie, or God herself showed up and granted you some wishes, what would you want? What people do you admire most? Then close your journal and put it aside for a day or two before continuing to the next step.

Karen wrote of her dream of a singing career. She pictured herself winning a Grammy Award and singing in cabaret clubs with the greatest jazz musicians.

4. EDIT YOUR LIST AGAIN. After your break, take a fresh look at what you've done. From the list of your present roles, choose the ones you still want and those you feel you must keep whether you want to or not. Then, from your "wish list" of roles you'd like, choose some you want to experiment with. This is the beginning of the "new you." Choose a few small, practical steps you can take to get some practice or experience in this new role, without taking a risk that's not comfortable for you.

Karen decided to try singing in several places, like her performance class, a karaoke bar, church, and as a volunteer entertaining in hospitals and senior centers. In this way she obtained some experience singing for an audience and experimented with putting an act together.

In the rest of the exercises in this book, you'll get other ideas about the "you" you like best. You'll build on what you've done here until you have redesigned and reshaped all the aspects of your life you want to change. You'll see that the exercises are written to help you gradually turn your dreams into reality.

A DIFFICULT MIDLIFE ROLE

Some of the role changes you are now experiencing will be voluntary, and some dictated by the passage of time. One particularly trying role for many women is that of caretaker for aging parents. You may still have children at home to care for, yet you are looking after your own parents as well. Balancing these responsibilities, along with those of a career, requires planning and support.

If your parents need your help, it is important to know how to provide it effectively. Juggling your own life, family, and career plus caring for a parent with dementia, chronic illness, or a life-threatening disease is very demanding. You will want to make the best decisions possible for your parents and yourself. If you read *The 10 Smartest Decisions a Woman Can Make Before 40*, the following guidelines will look familiar to you. I'm reiterating them here, adapted for you, because my clients find them so useful and because they are so pertinent to the needs of women in midlife.

Guidelines for Helping Family Members in Need

1. GET AS MUCH INFORMATION AS YOU CAN. Learn about the mental, physical, and emotional problems associated with your family member's condition, the extent of the help needed, and what is involved in the care. Often local agencies, such as a non-profit foundation for the particular disease or disability involved, will have lots of helpful information. You may also be able to get good advice and referrals from a senior citizen's center. If you have Internet access, take advantage of the many sites devoted to health-care concerns. You can search for information

and support groups on any subject, such as Alzheimer's disease or skilled nursing facilities. See the appendix of this book for some suggestions on where to begin.

2. INVOLVE YOUR ENTIRE FAMILY. Make sure everyone in your family is aware of the problem and knows what kind of help is needed. Don't let any reluctance to "bother" people, to tell the truth, or an old family relationship issue get in the way of utilizing all the support that everyone in the family can give. If you have five people who can share the financial burden, decision-making, and caregiving, you'll obviously have an easier time than if you try to do it alone.

3. LET EVERYONE CONTRIBUTE INDIVIDUALLY. Work to find a way for each family member to contribute help in the way that works best for him or her. As long as the burden feels fairly distributed in general, don't worry if one member contributes more time and another more money. It all qualifies as help, and an attempt to divide the labor "perfectly" will likely create a lot of friction.

4. HAVE REGULAR CAREGIVER DISCUSSIONS. Get everyone together regularly, at least once a month, to discuss how the arrangements are working, if everyone is doing his or her share, and how all the participants feel about it. Clearing the air frequently will prevent resentments from piling up.

5. USE COMMUNITY RESOURCES. Use as many community resources as you can find, especially if you're the only one caring for an elderly person. People often have negative feelings about senior

care residences or convalescent hospitals. If placing your family member in a good care facility is financially manageable and gives you a better opportunity to be emotionally supportive, however, this may well be a good decision. If your family member is at home, make sure you explore home health- or hospice-care options with your doctor, your medical insurance company, and community agencies.

6. FIND SUPPORT FOR YOURSELF. If you are caring for an elderly person with other family members, use your family meetings as times to air your frustrations and feelings and to support each other. If you are caring for a loved one by yourself, then let your friends know you'll need a lot of emotional support and allow them to help, or join a caregivers' support group.

7. TAKE BREAKS WHENEVER YOU CAN. A 1999 study in the *Journal of the American Medical Association (JAMA)* suggests that the stress of caring for a sick parent puts the caregiver's own health at risk. To keep your energy up, get enough sleep, eat well, exercise, and look after your own health. If you can manage to get away occasionally (one day a week, when the visiting nurse comes in, or rotate weekends off if possible), you'll be better equipped to handle the day-to-day pressure.

Changing places with parents is perhaps the most upsetting of the role changes you'll face. You lose your sense of security, of having someone you can run to in times of trouble, as well as losing a beloved member of your family. Make sure you have plenty of support and a place to express your feelings of grief and frustration.

RESTRUCTURING YOUR PRIMARY RELATIONSHIP

Facing the changes of maturity affects your connection with others as well. Your marriage or primary relationship will also evolve as your life changes.

Ruth is struggling with the changes created by her husband Paul's retirement. Although he thinks retirement and travel will be an idyllic time in their marriage, she is getting much more excitement from her growing career.

Like Ruth, you may be facing life-stage changes. If you and your husband have been focused on raising children or on your careers for many years, the loss of your central purpose can mean huge changes in your relationship.

Perhaps you have been married or in the same relationship for a long time and your connection feels stagnant or routine. You needn't accept this situation. With or without the cooperation of your partner, you can re-decide now how you want your relationship to be. What have you been missing? What routines would you gladly give up forever? If you take the time to decide what you want in your relationship—the aspects of it you want to keep and the aspects of it you want to change—you can present your ideas to your partner and more easily get cooperation in making the changes. Many of the decisions, checklists, and exercises in this book, which are designed to energize you, will help you to revitalize and energize your relationship as well. If you are married or in a primary relationship, it is crucial to share the thoughts and changes you are experiencing with your spouse. Discussing the results of your exercises will help to ensure that your new decisions are not only smart, but are mutually satisfying for both yourself and your partner.

SINGLE AFTER FORTY

According to the U. S. Census Bureau 1996 report:

> Half of American adults [77 million people!] are single, and the currently divorced population is the fastest growing marital status category—it has more than quadrupled from 1970. In 1996, 44.9 million adults age 18 and over had never been married, more than twice the number in 1970. Never-married adults accounted for 23 percent of all adults, and made up the largest share (59 percent) of the unmarried population in 1996, followed by those who were divorced (24 percent) and those who were widowed (18 percent). Sharp increases in the proportion never married have been primarily seen among men and women in their late twenties and early thirties. Between 1970 and 1996, the proportion of 25- to 29-year-olds who had never married more than tripled for women, from 11 percent to 38 percent, and more than doubled for men, from 19 percent to 32 percent. Among the 30- to 34-year-olds the proportion never married tripled from 6 percent to 21 percent for women, and from 9 percent to 30 percent for men.

The 1996 Census Bureau statistics show that "the number of unmarried-couple households (couples of the opposite sex) has grown sevenfold since 1970." Statistically, the older a woman gets, the more likely she is to be single. This is a fact of life, but being single doesn't have to mean being alone, and it doesn't have to be a permanent condition.

Single Is Not Solo

To have a full life, we all need other people. If you're a single woman over forty, you may be afraid that your closest relationships are in the past—but don't count on it. Many women report that the relationships they have later in life are the most valuable and pleasurable, whether they are intimate, committed partnerships, family connections, or friendships. In fact, there is nothing to prevent a single woman in midlife from deepening old relationships and creating new ones that can fill as much of her life as she likes.

Sally, who is enjoying travel, was worried about leaving her home, her pets, and her home-based business. As her business grew, she hired Barbara as an assistant. After a few months of working together successfully, Sally and Barbara agreed to share Sally's home. This has worked out well, because they are congenial roommates and business associates. Barbara and Sally arrange their schedules so that one of them is usually at home to feed pets, watch the house, and take care of the business when the other travels for business or pleasure.

Many women find that living together as roommates or in neighboring houses, condos, or apartments creates a companionship that is very supportive and satisfying.

Couples who find each other after forty often discover that their expectations are more realistic and their intimacy and relationship skills are better than when they chose a previous partner.

The new relationship is, therefore, more gratifying to them. As you let go of your responsibilities of caring for children, both you and a new partner can focus more on a relationship that meets your personal emotional needs.

A relationship begun now can face a future in which you enjoy the fruits of your previous labor, including financial security, emotional maturity, career success, freedom from parenting stress, and increased leisure time to pursue hobbies, dreams, travel, spiritual practices, and social causes. Even if you are still working on this security and freedom, you can begin to plan for your own future.

At sixty-three, **Julie** had been single all her life and had given up all thought of marriage, especially since she has had to care for her elderly parents. Then she met Ralph at a discussion group for caregivers. They began to have coffee together before meetings, and then to help each other with medical insurance forms, applying for programs for their parents, and eventually sharing some chores and errands. Much to their surprise, their relationship deepened, and now they're contemplating marriage. "At my age," says Julie with a smile, "I never thought I'd be considering marriage. But I know what a caring son Ralph is, and how responsible and honorable he is. I have seen him in real-life situations, and I trust him. My father's illness has been painful and stressful, but Ralph has been my comfort and solace. We actually find something to laugh about together every day."

If you regard the changes in life as you get older as opportunities to re-decide and try things you always wanted to do, you may find, as Julie has, that some wonderful new roles and experiences are waiting for you.

CHAPTER 3

Make Your Job a Joy: Decide to Revitalize Your Career, or Try a New One

To love what you do and feel that it matters—how could anything be more fun?

—Katherine Graham

As a woman over forty today, you probably have experience working outside the home. Today's financial conditions make it necessary for almost every woman to earn a living. If you're single, a single parent, or the head of your household, making an income is crucial.

Financial security is one foundation for a good, satisfying life. It is extremely important, and I will show you how to create it later in this book. In the year 2000, according to *U.S. News & World Report*, "... 4.7 million Americans—more than ever before and more than in the foreseeable future—will 'celebrate' their fortieth birthday. They are healthier, better educated, and have more opportunities than previous middle-agers. But they are also more financially insecure than their parents or older siblings were at this stage. ... They are working harder at their jobs, rushing home to care for younger children and older parents, and still trying to squeeze in a little age-defying exercise."

Work is much more than creating income and financial comfort. Working full-time consumes the majority of your waking hours each week. If you've been just putting in your time, not feeling fulfilled by your work, or if you're feeling stifled and bored, it may be time for a change.

SMALL CHANGES FOR BIG RESULTS

If you feel that you're stagnating at work, the easiest place to alleviate the problem is right at your job. You may be able to alter one or more aspects of your duties, which will bring a new spark to your work. Using the following guidelines, you can make changes that will refresh and invigorate your working experience.

Guidelines for Making Changes at Work

1. EVALUATE WHAT'S MISSING. If you're not happy or stimulated, if you're frustrated about lack of advancement, or if you feel unappreciated, explore your feelings and thoughts about your job. If you were happy in the beginning at your job, try and pinpoint when your feelings changed.

2. LOOK FOR THE SIMPLEST OPTIONS. Consider what choices you have in the company you work for. Does your company pay for education? Can you get trained for new skills? If you're having problems with a particular person in the workplace, can

you get help from your supervisor or employee assistance? Can you transfer to a different department or office?

Before **Sally** decided to strike out on her own as a consultant, she tried to change her situation at work to make it more satisfying. Because she really liked solving problems and turning bad situations around, she asked her company to reassign her to troubleshooting at the branch offices. Using her innovative abilities in this way increased her satisfaction for a while, but it also had the effect of proving to her that she would be competent as a consultant.

3. SHOW OFF YOUR ASSETS. Use your ability to make smart decisions and your other assets (which you will explore in the following exercise) to shine at your job. If you have skills you're not using on the job, find ways to offer to incorporate them into your work. For example, if you use a computer at home and not on the job, offer to learn the programs your company uses or to do a specific project on the computer. If you have an idea for improving profits or operations, write it up and present it to the appropriate manager.

When **Karen** began to help her co-workers with computer projects, the grocery-store manager heard about her expertise from other employees. Karen made some suggestions about improving the store's computer system to make it more useful to the cashiers, and he implemented her ideas. Later, when a supervisory position became available, he recommended Karen, which meant a substantial wage increase and other benefits for her.

4. BE BUSINESSLIKE. The seemingly casual attitude at work today is deceptive. Don't fall into the trap of Ally McBeal and other media images of the carefree working atmosphere. Keep your demeanor businesslike, even when others at your work are very casual. You don't have to be stuffy, but remember it's a place of business, not your family. Don't share too much personal information and keep your eye on the company's goals—the customer, the product, or profits. If you are serious and dedicated, you may not be included in the water-cooler conversations, but management will notice your professionalism. When the next promotion comes up, you'll be on the list.

Although **Marian's** co-workers for the legal registry tended to dress quite casually, she was always careful to dress in a businesslike manner. At the firms where she worked, she steered clear of office politics and gossip. When Marian began seeking a full-time position with some of those firms, the partners knew her image and demeanor were consistently businesslike.

5. UNDERSTAND THE CORPORATE AGENDA. Every business has its own agenda, and understanding your employer's will help you avoid frustration and even legal liabilities. This problem can be as simple as working for a badly managed company and being frustrated because you see it wasting money. Or it can be a more serious problem: you may work for a business that engages in dishonest practices. Understanding your corporate culture will prevent you from running afoul of unspoken and unwritten rules. If what is happening at your workplace is confusing, with rules or procedures that change frequently or

don't make sense, your company may have a hidden agenda that may make it an unpleasant, or even unsafe, place for you to work. Your personal ethics, moreover, could be at odds with the ethics of your employer. For example, you may believe in protecting the wilderness and your employer is a strip miner. To be a happy, comfortable employee, you may need to change jobs or industries.

6. BE REALISTIC ABOUT ADVANCEMENT. As a woman over forty, you probably know whether your company has a "glass ceiling" whereby women, people of color, or older people don't get promoted beyond a certain level. You need to decide for yourself whether it is worth trying to fight this type of policy, or whether you should find another place to work. Sometimes it is possible to help raise the consciousness of a workplace, through union activity or through personal discussions with people who have power. If you decide that you want to fight this aspect of corporate culture, however, you should be prepared for a real battle. You'll need financial and emotional support (the ACLU, NOW, AARP, or other organizations that have resources and know-how), information (available from the same groups), and a real dedication to making change. Obviously, taking your employer to task for discrimination is not generally viewed favorably by management, and even if you "win" your fight, you probably won't be a welcome team player. As alternatives, your could start your own business, or you could join another company where management shares your values.

7. DON'T TAKE ON TOO MUCH RESPONSIBILITY. One of the biggest sources of frustration for the women who come to me with work stress results from taking on more responsibility than they need to. Although it can be effective to make formal suggestions on how to streamline a process or improve a product, it is not necessary to solve every problem your company may have. If you don't own the company (and even if you do), you needn't devote all of your energy to its success. Your job is defined, and that is what you should focus on.

By the way, women who tend to take on too much responsibility in their work often succeed at running their own businesses—they have the foresight it takes to see what would improve a business and make it run better.

8. KEEP LOOKING. Never let your résumé get out-of-date while you're working. No matter how good your job is, there could be a better one out there, or your situation could change. Keep in touch with a good employment counselor and consider the opportunities that come up. Even if you don't find a better job, you'll be able to keep up on the salaries and benefits offered elsewhere in your industry. You'll be prepared for your next request for a raise.

9. ASK FOR RAISES AND PROMOTIONS. If you are due a raise, and no one has offered you one, don't hesitate to ask. If you have been surveying the job market in your field, you'll have a better sense of what demands are reasonable. Set yourself up for a raise by following a success at work by a request for more

money. If you are valuable to the company, and document your achievements when you make your formal request, you're more likely to get the raise you want.

Sally always kept her résumé current, and through her professional associations and other networks she often learned about new opportunities. Her income grew rapidly because she made several very beneficial moves to new companies, and when she negotiated her employment contracts or requested an increase, she had several options if her demands weren't met. Because her employers knew this, and valued her work, they usually complied with her requests.

THE RIGHT WORK FOR YOU

Even if you feel ready for a change in your work, you may not know what type of job you want to take. To make a change for the better, you'll want to base your decision to revitalize your career on knowledge of who you are and what will make you happy. By assessing your talents, skills, likes, and dislikes, you can form a picture of the kind of work that will give you success and satisfaction.

Job Evaluation

Your journal, beginning with the exercises you did in the first two chapters, can help you evaluate what kind of career adjustment or change would be best for you. Here you'll use it to explore your options and plan your strategy. This exercise is an opportunity to "try on" some career possibilities before you make any real changes.

Begin with your past and present job experience (if you have been a wife and mother, that is also work experience).

1. WRITE THE HEADING "SKILLS," ON A PAGE IN YOUR JOURNAL. On this page list all the skills you have acquired in your work history. Include management skills, such as overseeing schedules and budgets, and managing money, people, and time. Include whatever computer and technological skills you have. Don't leave out communication skills—do you teach, make presentations, have a sales record? Also include your organizational skills, which can run the gamut from maintaining good files to hosting a major promotional event. Finally, include your expertise: are you well versed in legal matters, accounting, education, trends, commodities?

Karen worked for a time as a waitress when she was getting her cashier training, so she has practiced the organizational skills and interpersonal skills that a demanding job requires. She also has developed skills as a single mother (budgeting, childcare, scheduling, tutoring, cooking/menu planning for health and nutrition, housecleaning, and the like) in addition to the skills she has learned at the workplace.

2. NOW TAKE A LOOK AT THE SKILLS YOU HAVE MASTERED. Think about combining them in different ways. For example, **Rose's** skills in relating to people as a hairdresser could be used in a business to maintain good client relations, and her experience in running her salon would be valuable in managing a private practice as a counselor.

3. DO SOME RESEARCH ABOUT POSSIBLE JOBS YOU COULD DO.
Attend a job fair, get career counseling at a local college career
center, and look at the classified Help Wanted ads. Talk to
people you know about their jobs—find out how they spend
their time at work, what they enjoy about their job, and what
they dislike.

4. EXAMINE BUSINESSES IN YOUR COMMUNITY. Check the yellow
pages for businesses that interest you and are compatible with
your skills, and learn as much as you can about them. When
you find a business that intrigues you, consider making an
appointment with the owner or an executive to learn more
about what the business does and how it works. Generally people are flattered that others are interested in them and their
business, and are happy to spend time with an enthusiastic listener. If you are comfortable doing so, you might offer to take
the individual out to lunch.

Karen, whose hobby has been working on a home computer
(which suited her odd hours), has helped her friends set up personal Web sites. By searching on the Internet and the yellow pages,
she found some Web site production and advertising companies
that sparked her imagination. She thought she'd like to combine
her experience as a single mother and her computer expertise to
create Web sites or other Internet advertising for women-owned
businesses. Karen was particularly interested in businesses that
offered something useful to single moms. She wasn't sure she wanted
to start a business of her own, but she decided to explore the jobs
available in that area.

Exploring other businesses that are compatible with your skills and expertise will give you new ideas and options for changing and expanding your career—you can decide to work for other businesses or even create your own.

START YOUR OWN BUSINESS?
WHY NOT?

After forty, both men and women worry about not being able to find or change jobs as easily as when we were younger. There seems to be a bias in today's technology-driven job market toward hiring younger people. Many employers consider younger people to be more adaptive and faster-paced than people with more experience. Working women are realizing that self-employment not only avoids the problem of age-conscious employers, but it also offers lots of flexibility, independence, and excitement.

The idea of having your own business may have been a long-awaited dream, or it may sound completely impossible to you. No matter how you feel about it now, after exploring your alternatives you may find that starting your own business is not only possible, but it's the best option available to you. Many women today have used their life experience, talents, and knowledge to create a service, a product, or a process they can sell to others.

"Women . . . now own more than 30 percent of the nation's sole proprietorships!" writes Carol Milano in *Hers: The Wise Woman's Guide to Starting a Business on $2,000 or Less*. "According to the National Foundation for Women Business Owners, between 1986 and 1997, women-owned businesses increased at nearly twice the national average. In the past decade, the number of woman-owned firms has grown by 78 percent."

Contrary to what you might think, starting your own business doesn't necessarily require a lot of cash. Milano offers "four features of a shoestring start-up," summarized here:

1. START YOUR VENTURE WITH AN OFFICE AT HOME. A home office keeps your costs down, and if you have children at home, you'll have the added advantage of having more time with them. In your own spare room, garage, basement, or even a corner of your kitchen, you can begin a business with very little risk, even while you're still working at another job.

2. CHOOSE TO OFFER A SERVICE RATHER THAN A PRODUCT. By offering a service, you avoid having to invest a lot of money in supplies or inventory. Most businesses owned by women are service businesses. Think about a service that local residents or businesses could use. If you are a good cook, you might find a need in your community for low-calorie meals, party catering, or take-home desserts. If you have computer, writing, or bookkeeping skills, you can offer a service to others who are not as adept. Running errands, organizing homes and offices, tutoring children, or teaching music, computer skills, or languages, are all quite simple businesses to begin. If you're artistic, think of a designing service or use sewing skills to offer alterations.

3. SELECT A BUSINESS REQUIRING NO COSTLY EQUIPMENT OR INVENTORY. Begin simply, with as little equipment as possible. If

more sophisticated equipment will improve your service, you can use your profits to acquire it gradually.

4. MAKE SURE THE BUSINESS IS SUITED TO LOW-COST ADVERTISING. Choose to begin your business locally, where you can advertise in small local papers, on bulletin boards, and by passing out flyers. After you have some experience in your business, you can expand to a larger, more expensive-to-reach market.

Many women-owned businesses, including Anita Roddick's The Body Shop, Mrs. Field's Cookies, and Martha Stewart, Inc., began as small enterprises, and later expanded to multimillion-dollar international corporations. The women who created all three of these huge businesses did what they knew, learned and grew as they went, and ultimately achieved great success.

In *No More 9 to 5: What to Do When You Can't Find a Job, Don't Want a Job, or Are Unhappy with the Job You Have,* author William Larson lists the three essential qualities of a successful business idea:

1. "IT SHOULD BE SOMETHING THAT INTERESTS AND EXCITES YOU." Being enthusiastic about your project will keep you energized enough to follow through.

2. "A DEMAND MUST EXIST OR YOU MUST CREATE ONE." Once you have an idea of what you'd like to do, you must research it to be sure there is a need or to find a way to interest people in what you offer.

3. "IT MUST BE SOMETHING YOU DO WELL." You may need to take some classes or find other ways to hone your skills, but doing

a good job is essential to getting repeat business and a good reputation. When your clients recommend you to their friends, you get cost-free (and very persuasive) advertising.

The Internet offers many new opportunities to begin your own business with nothing more than an idea. Women are offering Web site design services, auctioning goods online, and offering a wide variety of services via e-mail. This new technology is creating a business revolution!

BRAVE NEW WORLD: WORK IN THE NEW MILLENNIUM

In the last century, employment opportunities for women have grown from almost no choices to a nearly infinite variety of options. Women can work at almost any job, from the military to professional careers such as law and medicine. There may be some barriers to overcome, but with determination and motivation you can work at whatever you want.

Since the advent of computers, beepers, faxes, cell phones, and the Internet, more and more people have the opportunity to work at home, with flexible schedules, travel, and even multiple jobs. Telecommuting is an especially good idea if you are still caring for young children, because you can shape your hours to the needs of your children.

Once you know what kind of work you want to do, you may be able to arrange it in a new way by using the tools of the new millennium. For example, if you enjoy writing, you can write magazine and newspaper articles, advertising copy, business reports and brochures, and content for Web sites from your own home, and send them anywhere in the world.

If you're good with numbers, you can learn to do bookkeeping or prepare tax returns and financial data for yourself, for your clients, or for companies that need help.

If you'd like to represent a company, selling its products, you can stay in touch with customers and your company headquarters by cell phone and e-mail. Most businesses supply their sales representatives with laptop computers and cell phones for just this purpose.

The downside of all this technology can be that it's so easy to work at all hours that you can find work taking up all of your time. It's come as a surprise to many of us that with all the labor-saving and time-saving technology we have, we seem to be busier than ever. Because we can do more, we seem to expect more of ourselves; therefore an essential part of learning to use the technology is learning to manage it. The more freedom and independence you create for yourself, the more you'll need to learn to keep it all under control. Managing your time, putting all the aspects of your life into perspective, and creating balance are essential tasks at this stage of your life. In the following exercise, you'll picture your ideal working environment. As you do it, think about keeping your work and your personal life in balance.

Your Ideal Work

Ask a friend to read the following instructions as you follow them, or read them yourself into a tape recorder and play them back.

They should be read slowly, in a soft voice, allowing plenty of time to follow each instruction.

Sit in a comfortable chair, feet flat on the floor, and let your body relax. Close your eyes. Imagine it's a few years in the future and you're waking up on a workday. Allow the picture of this ideal day to unfold. You are looking forward to beginning work today. What is it you are looking forward to? You get out of bed. . . . How do you get ready for work? What do you wear? Do you have breakfast? How do you get to work? Where do you work? Are there other people involved? Describe them. What are you doing? Continue to go through the day, enjoying your work, observing what you do that pleases you. Pay attention to all the details. After your work is done for the day, visualize returning home and how you spend your evening. Is anyone there? What do you do?

Explore this ideal work and life as much as you like. When you're finished, write a description of your visualization in your journal. By observing your fantasy work life, you can draw conclusions about the adjustments you can make to your real life today to bring in elements of your fantasy.

When **Laurie's** therapist guided her through a similar visualization, she found that everything she imagined involved helping people in a very personal way. This helped her decide to use her medical training in hospice.

By exploring your feelings and your expertise, you can create a satisfying and sustaining career. Earning a living doesn't have to be dull or stressful. If you spend the majority of your daily hours in productive and fulfilling labor, work will become self-expression.

CHAPTER 4

The Buddy System: Decide to Focus on Friendship

When we see the look in another's eye that we are truly understood, we rest for a time with profound gratitude in that emotional oasis.

—Alice Clark

A positive connection with friends and family is the added ingredient that makes life enjoyable. You greatly enhance your experiences and achievements by sharing them with those closest to you. As you enter maturity, your friendships are what may make the difference between living a fulfilling life and being miserably alone. If you were raised in a traditional way, you may have been taught that your spouse and children should be the focal point of your social life, and if you are surrounded by a loving family, you are indeed fortunate. Of course, I don't advocate neglecting your spouse or children. As a mature woman today, however, your network of friends may be your best source of close and lasting relationships. As an increasing percentage of women decide to remain single, and people live farther away from their families, more and more people are turning to their friends for a feeling of connection.

In fact, studies have shown that a variety of social ties is good for us physically as well as emotionally. In *Toxic Friends, True Friends,* Florence Isaacs writes:

> Evidence strongly suggests that social ties defend us against illness in general, and, when we do get sick, they boost our odds of survival. The more friends you have—the more socially well-rounded you are—the longer you're likely to live. . . . Your network of friends, neighbors, co-workers, and other supportive people not only makes life easier, it boosts the odds you'll live longer, healthier, and happier. Social ties protect us from the stresses of life and from stress-related killers like heart disease, high blood pressure, and alcohol abuse.

MAKE NEW FRIENDS, KEEP GOOD FRIENDS

When you decide to focus on friendship, you bring all of the benefits mentioned by Isaacs into your life. Long-term friendships are wonderful and valuable, but if you don't make new connections as you get older, your group of friends may diminish due to death and relocation. Widening your web of friends is fun, and if you haven't made new friends in a while, updating your definition of friendship and increasing your skills at meeting people will be worth your while. I'll help you find ways to do both later in the chapter.

If all your friendships were formed many years ago, if you don't have enough friends to keep your life full and rewarding, or if you find yourself focused only on family, you'll find the following exercise enlightening.

Friendship Style Analysis

This exercise is an opportunity to examine your attitudes about giving and receiving friendship. You may be surprised by what you learn when you analyze your friendship style. First, find a quiet place to sit down with your journal.

1. GIVING FRIENDSHIP. What kind of friend are you? To become aware of your patterns of giving friendship, make a list in your journal of the ways you treat your friends. Try to be as specific as you can about the way you behave. "I am nice to them" is not as informative or useful in the later steps of the exercise as, "I listen to them and don't criticize." Title your list "Giving Friendship," and answer the following questions with as much detail as possible:

- How do you treat your friends?
      Are you attentive and helpful?
      Are you interested in what they have to say?
      Is your style very intimate, or more distant?
      Do you try not to hurt your friends' feelings?
      Do you make a point of being polite to your friends?

- How do you like to interact with your friends?
      Are you affectionate, or would you prefer a good conversation to a hug?
      Do you like to send greeting cards, letters, and e-mail?
      Would you prefer to talk on the phone, or meet for coffee?
      Do you like to be with several friends at once, or do you prefer one at a time?

Add as many other details as possible to your list about how you act with friends.

2. RECEIVING FRIENDSHIP. How do you like your friends to treat you? To become aware of your patterns of receiving friendship, consider how you like your friends to relate to you. It may differ from what you do for your friends. Title this list "Receiving Friendship," and as with the prior step, be specific. Write down, in as much detail as possible, how you like to be treated, using the following questions to guide you.

- How do you like to spend time with your friends?

  Do you like to be invited to go places?

  Do you enjoy having quiet time together?

  Do you like to get together often, or would you rather meet occasionally?

- What do you want from your friends?

  Do you like to be listened to?

  Do you want them to respect you and to keep their agreements?

  Do you like to get presents, cards, and letters, or is personal contact more important?

  Continue exploring in this manner until you have a clear picture of what you enjoy receiving from your friends.

3. COMPARE AND ANALYZE THE DIFFERENCES. Review your lists and compare the way you treat your friends, and vice versa. The objective is to learn more about friendship and what it means to you—not to be self-critical. Many people give differently

than they would like to receive: some send cards and letters, but prefer receiving phone calls. Some people enjoy listening to others, but are not particularly concerned about expressing themselves. This exercise will help you understand how you want to love and be loved.

At this point you may find that you want to add to or revise either one of your lists, because understanding your preferences may inspire you to change some of them. Make changes until you feel your lists are an accurate reflection of you and your preferences.

4. DEVELOP A NEW DEFINITION OF FRIENDSHIP. Using your comparisons, create a list called "My Ideal Definition of Friendship." If your examination of the other lists shows that you like having deep conversations with your friends, either in person or on the phone, you know that conversation is an important sign of caring to you. If you like to play golf, tennis, or hiking with friends, then sharing athletic activities is an important expression of caring for you. If you like hugging and lots of caring attention, then warmth and affection are important to you. Or you may like your friendships to be more formal so that you don't feel smothered. Based on what you've learned, this list should be an accurate description of your ideal friendship.

5. TRY OUT YOUR NEW DEFINITION. Now that you have a clear idea of the kinds of friendships you would enjoy, you can decide to create more of them in your life. This can be done in two ways:

- Make changes in your current relationships—ask your friends to participate in activities that you enjoy, and spend more time with the friends whose style of friendship best complements your own.

- Create new friendships—reach out to your co-workers, your neighbors, or church members and invite them to accompany you in a favorite activity or for coffee. As an alternative, you may want to join a discussion group focused on literature, film, or painting, or take a class in yoga or cooking. If you spend time with people who have similar interests, you will soon create new friends.

Guidelines for Making Friends

If you find that you don't have enough friends, use the following guidelines for making new ones. Of course, you can tailor these suggestions to your personal tastes.

1. GET A LIFE. If you want to meet people with whom you have something in common, do things on a regular basis that involve others. Activities can range from taking classes, joining hobby clubs, volunteering, playing a sport or game, hiking, or any pursuit that meets regularly. The people you meet will share your interests, and you'll have something to talk about and enjoy together.

2. FIND INTERESTING, FUN PEOPLE. Being involved in an ongoing activity and meeting with the same people on a regular basis

gives you an opportunity to get to know them before you decide to pursue a more personal relationship. When you find someone you think is particularly pleasant, spend a little time talking with him or her during or after your activity. Ask questions about the project you are working on, or share experiences and advice. If you both enjoy the conversation, you can offer to meet before or after the session for coffee. From there, you can begin to do more things together until you've established a pattern of friendship.

3. DON'T OVERLOOK THE PEOPLE YOU KNOW. While you're making new friends, don't forget the people you already know. Is there a favorite family member you'd like to see more often? Call him or her and suggest going for a walk or to lunch. Are there acquaintances at work, at church, in your neighborhood, involved in your child's (or your own) school, or elsewhere with whom you might develop a friendship? Consider reaching out to them. Let these people know that you'd like to share events and activities.

Friendship is crucial to your emotional, mental, and physical health. If you follow these steps, you'll find that it isn't as difficult as you think it is to make friends. In fact, I bet you'll discover that a lot of people really appreciate your efforts to befriend them.

YOUR VERY BEST FRIEND—YOU

Whether you realize it or not, the relationship you have with yourself sets the pattern for how you connect with others. By developing a nurturing way to relate to yourself, you create a personal experience of both giving and receiving friendship.

Best of all, you'll have greater trust in your decision-making ability when you recognize yourself as your own best friend. When you become comfortable with having a constructive inner dialogue, you can create an internal support system—you'll become more confident in your evaluations of your thoughts, feelings, and options. The following exercise explores how you treat yourself as a friend and builds on your discoveries in the previous exercise.

Developing Inner Friendship

I. GET OUT YOUR JOURNAL. Write answers to the following questions:

- How do you relate to yourself?

- Are you supportive of yourself?

- Do you seek your own opinion or ignore it?

- Do you consciously talk over decisions with yourself before you make them, or just worry ineffectually about them?

- Do you enjoy time with yourself, or avoid being alone?

- Do you celebrate your accomplishments and successes?

- Do you motivate yourself to do well?

- Do you tend to criticize everything you do?

- Add any other aspects of how you relate to yourself.

2. COMPARE YOUR OWN INTERNAL RELATIONSHIP WITH YOUR DEF-
INITION OF FRIENDSHIP. You may be dismayed to find out that
you treat yourself quite differently from the way you treat your
friends. You might keep promises to a friend but often renege
on promises you make to yourself. You may not treat yourself
with kindness and respect. Perhaps you mentally "nag" or criticize yourself. You may never break a date with a friend, but
keep putting off time for yourself. The best test of your friendship with yourself is this: if someone else treated you the way
you treat yourself, would you want to be her friend?

3. BECOMING A FRIEND TO YOURSELF. In the previous exercise, you
discovered the kind of friendship you enjoy. Now that you have
compared your way of having an "external" friendship with your
way of having an "internal" friendship, you have more work to
do. Decide to improve the way you treat yourself and put your
decision into effect by developing simple ways of doing so.

One way to approach this task is to treat yourself as you would
treat a good friend. Ask yourself, "What would I do for Maggie if
she were in my shoes? What would I say to her?" It's likely that
you're usually more kind to her than to yourself. How would you
speak to your friend if you thought she forgot to do something?
Do you treat yourself more harshly? By comparing the way you
treat yourself with the way you treat your friends, you will begin

to develop clear guidelines about how to be your own friend. Write down your ideas about befriending yourself and put them into action.

Julie decided to spend twenty minutes each day having tea in her backyard among her beloved flowers, to choose one thing each week she wanted to do for herself, such as a facial, and to take a few minutes each morning to give herself a pep talk.

4. TO DEVELOP TRUST, BE CONSISTENT. You must be consistent in order to create an internal bond and a strong habit of being a good friend to yourself. Always treat yourself with care and consideration. Create a list of guidelines for your internal friendship and post it where you can see it often. Renew your plan for being a better friend to yourself every week for at least six weeks. With consistent practice, you'll find that treating yourself well becomes much easier and feels more comfortable.

Being a good friend to yourself is really not selfish. You'll discover that if you maintain your internal friendship, it becomes easier to be a good friend to others and to recognize when others are good friends to you.

YOUR FRIENDSHIP WITH YOUR PARTNER

Many of us don't think of our spouses or primary partners as "friends," but friendship is a basic element of a good relationship. Spouses who regard each other as friends report greater marital satisfaction and demonstrate the ability to comfortably share the responsibilities of their lives. And they have more fun—these partners know how to fill their days together with humor, caring, and good conversation. Now is a great time to learn to foster the friendship aspect of your marriage.

Your Relationship Reservoir

Every couple has a history of shared events and feelings, which I like to call their "relationship reservoir." If a couple has filled their reservoir with power struggles, nasty arguments, and broken trust, they have little to draw on when times are hard. On the other hand, a couple who has a history of trust, partnership, and kind and loving words and actions, has built up a lot of resilience and strength. Here are some guidelines to make sure your reservoir is storing what you need.

Guidelines for Creating a Relationship Reservoir

To create a positive atmosphere of caring between yourself and your spouse or primary partner, follow these steps:

1. ACCENTUATE THE POSITIVE. Make a conscious effort to notice your partner's strengths and good qualities. Repeat in your mind the attributes of your partner that you most like. If you are supportive of one another and work together to create a positive outcome for each other, your love and trust will grow daily. Work toward eliminating nasty remarks and criticisms of each other. If you cannot agree about behaviors you would like to see each other change, see a counselor, alone or together.

2. DO SOMETHING CARING EVERY DAY. It is so easy to take your partner for granted. Try a new approach. Remember to thank your partner for whatever he has contributed to the relationship on a daily basis. Leave a pleasant note, take the time to share a joke, hug, kiss, or a kind word. Such things seem insignificant, but over years of being together they will fill your reservoir with good will and a strong bond. (And I bet your spouse will delight you by responding in kind.)

3. KEEP THE LINES OF COMMUNICATION OPEN. Have a "state of the union" meeting at least once a week, in which you discuss your feelings and the problems facing you, and work together toward solutions. If you share your concerns on a regular basis, they will not grow to a point of contention. Your meeting will be most effective if it also includes a discussion of the things that are going well. Set your meeting up to be a "date," with breakfast in bed, a nice dinner out, or a special candlelit meal at home. Even sharing takeout food can be a lovely opportunity to "catch up" with each other and add one more good memory to your reservoir.

4. KEEP A "MEMORY BOOK" OF YOUR RELATIONSHIP. Over the years, your book will become more and more meaningful as a reminder of the best parts of your relationship. Include a few photos of important events, notes and cards you have sent one another or received from friends and family, and notations of especially kind acts, thoughtful words, and loving interactions during your history together. Women often have a keepsake book of memorabilia from their wedding or a scrapbook of

items concerning their children. Your memory book serves a similar purpose. Like a condensed version of many photo albums or videos, this one book will give you instant access to the highlights of your time together. Looking through it together can give your relationship a boost whenever you feel the need.

DEVELOPING FRIENDSHIPS WITH YOUR CHILDREN

As a mother, it is hard to believe how quickly children grow up to become independent, mature adults. Your role changes from the caretaking, responsible parent to a more equal position of friend and advisor. Treating your children as friends will help make this transition smoother. Of course, young children need parents who are not reluctant to take charge and enforce rules and standards, but as a parent you can also treat them with kindness and respect, encouraging them to think for themselves. As your children mature, it becomes less important to enforce rules and much more important to emphasize your friendship. If all goes well, your relationship will evolve into a much more equal, adult-to-adult connection. One of the great joys of parenthood is seeing a child grow into a responsible adult and sharing life as friends.

I have taught the following guidelines to many different people for years. In *The 10 Smartest Decisions a Woman Can Make Before 40,* I included similar guidelines devised to help a young woman develop an adult relationship with her family. This version is adapted for your use.

Guidelines for Helping Your Children Grow into Friends

1. CALL YOUR GROWN CHILDREN BY THEIR GIVEN NAMES, RATHER THAN CHILDISH NICKNAMES. If you have teenagers, they may already have asked you to do this. "Suzie Q"–type nicknames are fine for small children, but as children grow up, they feel more respected when called by their given names. By doing so, you also remind yourself to treat your children as young adults.

2. DISCUSS ADULT TOPICS. As your children grow, don't limit your conversation strictly to family topics or questions about their personal life. Involve them in discussions of current events and the like, just as you would with a friend. Take a minute to think of "adult" topics you'd like to talk about with them. Politics, events, sports, work issues (just facts and events—avoid complaining), or local neighborhood issues are all suitable subjects.

   Nagging and constant reminders are ineffective with young children and inappropriate with grown children. Of course, you should set limits and make sure that irresponsibility and bad behavior have consequences, but you needn't patronize your children. If they want something from you, don't respond unless they ask you in a polite, adult manner. Include them in your planning discussions and expect that they will take appropriate responsibility for family issues.

3. SHARE WITH YOUR GROWN-UP CHILDREN ON A PARENT-TO-PARENT BASIS. If your children have children of their own, you have expertise they can benefit from, but be willing to learn from them as well. If they're reading books or taking courses

on parenting, discuss the information as you would with another parent your own age. If they parent their children differently than you did, don't take it as a personal affront and don't offer advice unless you're asked to.

4. DON'T REACT IF YOUR GROWN CHILD DOES OR SAYS SOMETHING ANNOYING. Just ignore it and change the subject. Treat your adult children as politely as you would the grown children of a friend. If they are doing something to annoy you and you don't react, they will stop. After all, if you were with a friend's family, and someone did something odd, you'd just ignore it and wouldn't let yourself be drawn into a family squabble. You'd just be polite and pleasant, for your friend's sake.

5. ASK YOUR CHILDREN FOR THEIR OPINIONS AND ADVICE. Even in early childhood, children can be encouraged to develop their own opinions about events and decisions you face as a family. As they get older, you can ask for their ideas about what to do. When your children become adults, you can request advice about work issues, investments, or other concerns. Sharing advice as friends and equals will create the friendly connection you want.

6. PAY ATTENTION TO THE BALANCE OF YOUR INTERACTION. As a parent, the role of nurturer and caretaker is familiar, and perhaps comfortable, for both you and your children. But you don't want to foster that relationship when your children are grown. Don't let your part in the relationship slide into all giving (or all receiving). Remember, the objective is to create a

friendship with your children. If your children always seem ready to take from you, make some suggestions of what they can do in return.

After following these guidelines for a few months, your interactions with your children will change, and you'll be able to relax and be your adult self. You'll have more fun with your children when all of you are interacting as friends and equals.

FAMILY AS FRIENDS

In addition to your partner and your children, you can also become better friends with your siblings and other family members. Try changing the way you have interacted with these people in your past. Use the information in the "Friendship Style Analysis" exercise (see page 93) to find some new activities to explore. If you've had difficulty getting along with a family member and you can't resolve it on your own, get help from a therapist. Although it's not realistic to expect to be best friends with all of your relatives, looking at them from a new perspective may surprise you. Think of each person separately, as an individual. You may be overlooking a great friendship right in your own family.

THE VALUE OF CASUAL FRIENDS

Some people become friends because circumstances bring them together. Perhaps you worked with someone and ate lunch together fairly often, but when one of you left the job, the friendship didn't survive. Or you were quite friendly with a neighbor who moved away, and your contact ended.

You probably know what's like to get together with a close friend who you haven't seen for a long time. It's as though you were never apart. Your connection is based on many shared experiences, values, and feelings, and it remains strong. Circumstantial friendships don't provide the same type of bond, but that doesn't mean they're not valuable.

It's likely that when you enter a new environment, you will meet people you enjoy, but don't feel a deep connection to. These friendships are like pleasant conveniences, where both parties benefit by the contact, but neither has the interest to pursue the friendship further. The relationship may feel vaguely uncomfortable or wrong, as if there is something "false" about it.

Mary enjoys having lunch with other teachers at work, chatting with them about classroom problems and lesson plans, and she even meets another teacher before class to exercise. But when she began teaching at a new school, those friendships were replaced by connections with teachers in her new location.

There is no need to feel guilty if one or more of your friendships feels circumstantial. It is very helpful for both of you to have one another at this moment; you can enjoy whatever you share and move on when it's over. Most likely your friend has similar benign feelings of friendship toward you, and the parting is not more than mildly sad for either of you. Don't deprive yourself of this pleasant contact because it doesn't meet some expectation, and don't try to force it to be more than it is. There's no reason to back away from a temporary, congenial connection.

CIRCLES OF FRIENDS

Every friendship is different, and you deserve to have a full spectrum of friends in your life. You can picture your friendships as a series of concentric circles, one inside the other. At the outermost circle are the people you like but haven't gotten to know well—folks you've met at work, church, or other groups; friends of friends and other pleasant acquaintances. Some of these people will never be closer to you than they are now. Some of them, however, become closer to you and move into the next circle. These are people you see fairly often and like quite a bit. They may be circumstantial friends who are meaningful to you at the time, but who don't stay around. Or they may be members of a group you spend time with, but not special friends of yours. If you're particularly fond of a casual friend, it's worth your while to make an effort to get closer. Let an acquaintance know you'd like to have more personal contact by inviting him or her to coffee after a meeting or to a party at your house.

Perhaps your relationship will move into the third circle—developing friends. You'll both take the opportunity to know each other better and learn whether you have much in common. With some effort, and some luck, the friendship may eventually move into the fourth circle—close friends. It usually takes some time for a relationship to develop this far, but when it does, you both will share a long-term connection.

Mary made one friend among the teachers in her last school. She and Susan started talking on the phone in the evenings, and when Mary began to question her future options, she felt safe confiding in Susan. As they talked, they became closer, and Mary found Susan's support and advice very helpful. Years later, in separate schools, they were still friends.

Nothing enriches life like friendships. You probably remember the old adage, "Make new friends, but keep the old. One is silver, and the other gold." As your life develops after forty, you'll learn how true that is. "Although some people are content with a few friends," advises Isaacs in *Toxic Friends, True Friends,* "and although there are costs to friendship, such as time and obligations, a variety of connections means more opportunities to grow. The more friends you have, the more options and choices you have, and the better your chances of getting your needs met. If one friend isn't available, someone else is."

With plenty of friends around, you can make sure that you get your full measure of delight, support, and companionship.

CHAPTER 5

An Apple a Day: Decide to Stay Healthy

What we must keep remembering is that our bodies respond to the feminine principle, the goddess. They respond to rest, to nurturing, to a presence that says you are okay just the way you are.
—Dr. Christiane Northrup

Accovrding to the most recent National Vital Statistics Report, a woman born in 1900 had a life expectancy of 50.7 years, and if she survived to age forty, that expectancy increased to 72.68 years. For a woman born in 1960, life expectancy at birth is 73.24, and life expectancy at age forty is 80.9 years. We are living longer, but if we want to live healthier and more productive lives, we have to invest in our mental and physical well-being.

You may not have thought about it, but at forty you become an "apprentice senior citizen." From this point on, everything you do determines how healthy you will be as a senior. If you want to enjoy your "golden years," you'll make becoming healthy and staying that way a priority. There's a strong chance that you've spent more time caring for the health and well-being of others than for yourself. And after forty, you become part of the "sandwich generation"—women who are taking care of children and ill or aging parents.

Julie has no children of her own, but several of her friends are caring for parents as she is, and taking care of their children too. She's stressed enough with her responsibilities, and she wonders how her friends handle their double load. Julie and her friends share resources and provide each other with emotional support.

If you want to optimize your quality of life in the later years, it is imperative to minimize and release stress, as well as maintain a healthy, active lifestyle.

LOOK FORWARD TO A HEALTHY FUTURE

When it comes to your physical health, the most important advice you can get is from your doctor. Now is the time to have a complete physical. Arrange a regular schedule of physical exams, mammograms, and Pap smears, performed annually, or as often as your doctor recommends.

University of Chicago researcher Michael Roizen, M.D., has done a thorough survey of lifestyle factors that affect your health for his book *Real Age: Are You as Young as You Can Be?* Roizen writes: "I believe the difference between your calendar age and your real age results largely from your health behaviors." He maintains that you can lower your physiological age ("your real age") by taking the following steps:

- If you are an adult with no history of bleeding problems or other contraindications to aspirin, take an 80- to 325-mg tablet every day to help keep your arteries free from clots and reduce the incidence of certain kinds of colon cancer.

- Floss and brush your teeth daily. The bacteria that cause periodontal disease appear to trigger inflammation throughout the body, including the arteries.

- Both vitamins E and C seem to help keep arteries clear. Take a 400 IU vitamin E tablet daily, and three times a day eat food containing vitamin C.

- Have sex. It decreases stress and helps enhance intimacy. [This is probably one reason that research shows happily married couples live longer, healthier lives.]

- Eat breakfast every day. Studies show an association between breakfast-eating and longevity.

- Get a dog. Dog owners stay young longer, possibly because they get exercise caring for their pet.

- If you smoke, quit.

- Eat a varied, healthy diet, including tomato sauce and plenty of fresh vegetables, for their anti-cancer properties.

- Exercise regularly. Keep active by walking, dancing, swimming, or playing sports.

- Have friends. Research shows that people who are socially active and connected are healthier and live longer.

Whether you follow Dr. Roizen's advice or your own doctor's, make a plan for creating and maintaining optimum health and stick to it.

EXERCISE YOUR BRAIN AND BODY

Most people today understand that physical activity is beneficial to the mind and body. Fewer individuals realize that our brains also need exercise for optimum health. If you want to be as healthy as possible for your whole life, it is essential that you keep both your body and your mind active.

For many of us, finding the time to exercise is easier said than done. Family responsibilities and career ambitions tend to crowd personal activities out of our schedules. In the following pages, I'll look at some ways to make healthy physical and mental activity a regular part of life.

Staying (or Getting!) in Shape Can Be Fun

Many of the women over forty who come to see me are intimidated by the exercise advice that they get from magazines and the media. Like them, you may not be comfortable joining a gym or taking aerobics classes. There are, however, other ways to get healthy exercise and have fun while you're doing it.

When **Rose** worked as a hairdresser, she was on her feet all day. Now, working as a counselor, she is quite sedentary. She finds the idea of "working out" unappealing. "All that 'jock stuff' turns me off," she says. "My idea of a great time is a stimulating conversation over lunch. I get very discouraged about staying fit."

Research shows that gardening, dancing, walking, yoga, and other forms of movement are just as effective for fitness purposes as the "jock" activities, and if you enjoy them more, you'll do them more. You might feel more motivated to exercise if you think of the "apprentice senior citizen" concept, and remember that you're exercising to keep your body young, supple, and useful, rather than trying to keep your weight down or attain some unrealistic ideal shape.

"Trying to lose weight," says **Rose**, "just upset me, and took all the pleasure out of eating and social occasions. But when I switched my focus to creating a healthier lifestyle, I began by walking with friends in the park. I take a tai chi class early in the morning, which feels like meditation rather than exercise, and I stopped worrying about weight issues. Now I just try to make healthier choices when I eat and stay active doing things I enjoy. I feel more alert, and my muscle tone has improved."

A Workout for the Mind

Current research indicates that mental and physical exercise work together to keep you alert, active, and healthy. According to RealAge.com, a University of Chicago Web site that compiles research on health, "Flexing your mental muscle often can help you live longer." The Web site also reports that:

> Scientists in the Netherlands found that people with the best memory skills and ability to process and deal with new problems have the lowest mortality rates—regardless of other health factors. The good news is that you can learn these skills at any age. Regular mental exercise, including

reading, performing tasks with your non-dominant hand, playing word and memory games, and participating in new activities will help your brain stay young.

Research conducted at several universities shows that it's never too late to improve your brain power. Even if you have had a lifetime of relative inactivity, starting an aerobic activity such as walking can improve your brain power as well as your muscle tone. When you walk or dance, for example, the increased circulation brings more oxygen to the brain as well as the rest of the body. In turn, the mind becomes more alert and remains sharper over time.

Neurobiologist and researcher Lawrence C. Katz, Ph.D., recommends other ways to help your brain stay young in his book, *Keep Your Brain Alive: 83 Neurobic Exercises to Help Prevent Memory Loss and Increase Mental Fitness*. Dr. Katz suggests the simple mental exercises summarized here:

1. CHALLENGE YOUR SENSE OF TOUCH. Place small objects such as paper clips, nails, and screws in a cup. Close your eyes and identify them by touch. This causes your brain to use different pathways than it usually does and keeps it active.

2. VARY YOUR ROUTINE. Get dressed after breakfast instead of before, or eat dessert first. According to Dr. Katz, brain-imaging studies show doing things in new ways activates large areas of the brain cortex.

3. USE YOUR NON-DOMINANT HAND. If you're right-handed, try brushing your teeth with your left hand. If you've ever had

your arm in a cast, you understand how using the other hand is a brain workout.

4. SMELL THE VANILLA. If you associate waking up with smelling coffee, teach your brain a different association. Cut a piece of sponge, saturate it with a fragrance such as vanilla, and sniff it when you wake up. New associations give you a fresh new feeling.

5. MOVE SOMETHING. You can stimulate your brain by doing something as simple as putting your wastebasket in a new location for a few days or rearranging the things in your desk drawers.

Doing crossword puzzles, playing Scrabble with friends, or learning something new are all ways to keep your brain alive and healthy. Try mastering a new language (or brushing up on high-school French), taking up bridge or chess, or taking a class in great films. You'll not only have fun, but you'll be mentally stimulated and make some social contacts all at once.

Another fun way to challenge your intellect is through music. "Making music engages the brain at all levels," maintains behavioral neuroscientist Norman M. Weinberger of the International Foundation for Music Research. Learning to play an instrument is an activity that involves the senses of touch, sight, and sound; requires symbolic interpretation, abstract thinking, and planning; and hones motor skills. It's the equivalent of taking your brain to the gym.

Karen, who loves jazz and attends concerts frequently, realizes that many vocalists retain their singing abilities until very late in life. The great Ella Fitzgerald sang almost up until her death, and many jazz and classical musicians have performed through a venerable old age. Karen knows that performing and learning new pieces of music takes a lot of mental concentration.

If you have musical talent or would like to develop a musical skill, there are plenty of classes for adults (even beginners). As an alternative you can join your church choir, or the Sweet Adelines— the national ladies' barbershop singing group.

Dancing of all kinds—social ballroom- , square- , or folk-dancing, ballet, tap, belly, jazz, or just "shakin' your booty" to a good beat—gives you some of the mental benefits of music as well as a healthy physical workout.

Staying mentally and physically active guards against depression and burnout. Research is beginning to indicate that even Alzheimer's disease can be prevented or delayed by an active mind. To ensure that you have a happy life after forty, decide to take care of your body *and* your intellect.

STRESS REDUCTION

Stress is a normal fact of life, we all encounter it, and years of negative stress can be debilitating. Learning to de-stress is essential to maintaining optimum health. If your work is stressful, if you're a single parent or a caretaker for your own elderly parent, or if you're grieving for someone you love, you're undoubtedly experiencing a high level of stress. It's not reasonable to try to avoid stress altogether, so the answer is to find ways to counteract and release the pressure.

"We're all trained as children in the basics of reading and writing, but we're not taught about stress management," writes psychologist Robert Epstein, Ph.D. in *Psychology Today.*

Close to 90 percent of visits to primary-care physicians are for stress-related problems. As many as 750,000 Americans attempt suicide each year, often because of unmanageable stress. . . . Fully 40 percent of employee turnover is stress-related. Recent studies show that stress weakens our immune system, increases our risk of heart disease and cancer, impairs our mood and performance, disturbs our sleep, contributes to sexual dysfunction, destroys relationships and generally makes us miserable.

Guidelines for Reducing Stress

There are many physical, mental, and emotional ways to lighten the burden. Here are some of the best.

1. DON'T BE PERFECT. "Perfectionist thinking patterns create stress, which in turn wreaks havoc on the body as well as on the mind," reports a study by psychologists J. Clayton Lafferty and Lorriane Coletti-Lafferty. "Perfectionists were found to have a 75 percent greater tendency to suffer from a variety of ailments, from headaches to depression to cardiovascular problems." If you relax your standards to a more realistic level, you'll also reduce your stress.

2. LISTEN TO MUSIC. "Research has confirmed the ability of music to decrease the effects of stressful stimuli," reports RealAge.com. "In several recent studies, music was shown to reduce heart and respiratory rates and decrease depression and fatigue. Keep a few relaxing CDs or tapes in your car, at work,

or wherever you feel the most stress. You never know when you'll need to find harmony."

3. EXERCISE. A walk in the park or on the beach, yoga, tai chi, dancing, or movement of any kind that you enjoy, including playing sports, will help you relax.

4. GET OUT INTO NATURE. Spending time in natural surroundings is a time-honored and proven way to restore your sense of well-being. Spending a weekend in the country or tending your flower beds or even your houseplants will relax and restore your spirits. The quiet and regular rhythms of nature are healing after the noise and rush of modern life.

5. MAKE A DATE. Enjoying time with your friends is one of the most pleasant ways to shake off the stress of a busy week. **Rose** meets a friend every Saturday morning for a long walk through the woodland trails of a local nature center, and then they have a light, healthy lunch at their favorite tearoom. They get social contact and exercise at the same time. Even a phone call can lighten the tension of a busy day, and friends can often offer advice that makes stressful situations easier to handle.

6. LAUGH. When you're rounding up your friends, include some who like to laugh. "Humor," advises RealAge.com, "helps relieve pent-up tension, and, by doing so, serves as a defense mechanism against stress." What could be more fun than reducing stress by laughing with your friends?

7. MEDITATE. Learning one of the many techniques of meditation gives you practice in calming your mind and controlling your

thought patterns. Some methods, such as *zazen* sitting meditation, can take years to master, but others are surprisingly simple. In *Meditation Made Easy*, Lorin Roche, Ph.D., recommends the following method for getting up in the morning: "Sit up, close your eyes, and stretch for a full minute, inhaling and holding each breath for ten seconds. Move whichever way your body wants. Doing this basic yoga move, called Yawn to Wake Up, will make you feel alert and in synch with yourself."

8. CURL UP WITH A GOOD BOOK. Reading fiction or non-fiction that absorbs your attention and draws you away from your everyday experience is like taking an instant vacation. It provides the same sort of mental change of environment that you get from going to a new location and can be a quick and easy little "getaway." Any book that you enjoy, from an old favorite like *Gone With the Wind*, to a biography of one of your personal heroines, will work this magic.

9. PAMPER YOURSELF. Schedule time for your favorite method of indulging yourself. Whether you like a warm bubble bath, a brief nap, a facial, or a massage—whatever feels pleasurable and self-indulgent to you is an effective antidote to stress. A small bottle of skin lotion in your favorite luxurious scent may seem expensive, but smoothing it over your skin, delighting in the scent and feel, can provide a very big pay-off in stress-reduction dividends.

10. BECOME THE MASTER OF YOUR TIME. We have all learned to live at a very rapid pace. With the Internet, and our involvement in a world economy, we could find ourselves working around the

clock. Expectations are high, and there never seems to be enough time for all you want to do. If you look carefully at what you're *really* doing, however, you may find that a lot of your time is wasted performing undesirable or unnecessary tasks. If you feel overloaded and stressed about time, try going on a "time budget." Turn off the TV unless there's something specific you want to watch—don't just sit in front of it. Limit your time on the computer, especially with e-mail and the Internet, two time-absorbers. If friends are e-mailing you silly jokes you don't enjoy, ask them to please take you off their group lists. Delete advertising mail without reading it. If you receive phone calls that are not important to you, pleasantly get off the phone. You can devote the time you save to some of the other stress-busters on this list.

II. COUNT YOUR BLESSINGS. Perhaps the simplest way of changing your mental outlook is to remind yourself of all that you already have. Just reviewing how far you've come, what you have accomplished, and what you have learned will encourage and soothe you. Appreciating your favorite possessions, your dearest friends, your closest family members, and yourself is something you can do anytime or anyplace.

Julie's group of fellow caretakers support each other in staying healthy. They get together to meditate, do yoga, and hike, which helps them to reduce stress. They also gather for dinner once a month. The members take turns making a large casserole or a batch of soup to share with one another, which eases everyone's burden of cooking. Julie wouldn't miss these evenings because they are such a relief for her.

RETHINK YOUR DIET

As you grow older, your physical needs change. In *Parade* magazine, Earl Ubell observed:

> Your body changes each decade—so fast in your early years that you wonder where 'the old you' went, so gradually in your later years that you scarcely notice becoming another person. "For most of us, our body weight creeps up between ages forty and sixty, initiating 'middle-aged spread.' Our metabolism—the process by which our bodies burn energy—slows down now, so our bodies are burning fewer calories. Much of that extra weight—and danger—also comes from less activity and taking in more high-fat foods and alcohol."

Rose knows all too well how true this is. Stepping up her physical activities has really made her feel stronger, but she also focuses on good nutrition. Rose makes sure she eats foods that are high in fiber and calcium, as well as whole grains and fresh produce and fruits. She monitors the amount of meat and fatty foods that she consumes.

Because of the hormonal and physical changes that come with midlife, you may need to alter lifelong habits of diet, nutrition, and exercise. Whatever dietary changes you decide to make, you're much better off if you follow good nutrition guidelines and adopt a healthy, varied diet. Dietary fads, such as the high-protein diet, diet drinks, or those that follow strict menus, are neither practical nor likely to work. "The fourth law of the universe is that for every diet, there is an equal and opposite binge," writes Geneen Roth, bestselling author of *Feeding the Hungry Heart*. "Diets aren't free. You will rebel, and when you do, you will gain more weight than you lost."

Similarly, in *The Unofficial Guide to Dieting Safely,* registered dietitian Janis Jibrin writes: "I do my best to convince you not to diet, at least not in the traditional, severely calorie restrictive fashion. If dieting kept your weight off over the long haul, I'd promote it. But it doesn't."

"No matter how large you are or how low your spirit is," advises Jill Podiasek, registered nurse and author of *The Ten Habits of Naturally Slim People,* "decide to step out of the process of dieting and into the process of health." A lifestyle you can stick to, with more exercise and a well-balanced diet, may not make you model-slim, but it will make you a lot healthier and happier.

Rose tried many diets and weight-loss programs in the years since reaching age thirty, when she first noticed she was gaining weight. Each of them seemed to make the problem worse. When she decided not to worry so much about weight, and opted instead for a healthy lifestyle, she was more motivated and much more successful at keeping weight off.

PERIMENOPAUSE AND MENOPAUSE

If you're forty or older and feeling depressed and tired, your malaise could be related to hormonal changes. Many women don't realize the changes we face before there's a noticeable difference in the menstrual cycle. Perimenopause is the condition preceding the end of menstruation. These physical and emotional changes include irregular periods, night sweats, hot flashes, mood swings, and difficulty concentrating, and are relatively common in women as young as thirty-five.

Your doctor can help you determine if you've entered peri-menopause by performing a simple blood test. The test measures the amount of follicle-stimulating hormone (FSH) that your body is producing. Because women's hormonal changes vary, however, the test can't tell you how far along you are in the process or when you will complete menopause and no longer have periods.

Rose has been concerned about her health. She's been stressed, because in addition to working full-time she's earning hours toward her counseling license by going to school on the weekends. She really loves both school and her clinical work, and she didn't understand why she was so tired and depressed. She had regular psychotherapy and supervision as a part of her practicum, so she knew her problem wasn't simply emotional. When she began having heavier menstrual flow, she became really worried. "I was so relieved when I went to my gynecologist and Dr. Talbot told me it was perimenopause. I could understand that; it was some-thing I could handle. Dr. Talbot prescribed low-dosage hormone-replacement therapy that regulated my periods and my mood. I feel fine now, and I'm as enthusiastic as ever. Dr. Talbot says this low-dose HRT will slow my progress into menopause and make the symptoms mild and more gradual. I'm so relieved."

If you find that your reactions to events are more dramatic than you're used to, or you're feeling more tired than seems war-ranted, your hormone levels may be changing. By the time you are forty, it is important to have your doctor monitor your hormone levels. Although the majority of women pass through perimenopause and menopause without serious problems, there are related health considerations to discuss with your physician. You may need help mitigating hot flashes, muscle aches, vaginal dryness, loss of libido, or mood swings. It is even more important, however, to address other long-term health issues connected to changing hormonal levels. Preventing osteoporosis, heart disease, and high blood pressure is essential after forty, and it's one of the most important things you can do to keep healthy.

There is an ongoing debate among researchers and physicians about the advantages and drawbacks of hormone replacement therapy. Some experts advocate the use of HRT, others recommend natural supplements. There is conflicting research as to whether HRT prevents heart disease and osteoporosis. To make an informed decision about a course of hormone treatments that is right for you, consult your physician and have regular physicals and blood tests.

By making smart decisions about your health now, you can increase the odds that your life after forty will be active, healthy, and fun. You have many years ahead of you—make sure they're the best that they can be.

CHAPTER 6

Take It to the Bank: Decide to Secure Your Financial Position

The most popular labor-saving device is still money.
—Phyllis George

Now is the time to decide to create financial security for yourself. Most women in midlife look forward to leisure activities such as traveling or pursuing interests they never had time for. If you dream of retirement, it is never too early to prepare. Even if you feel that it's too late, or your income is too small, there are always steps you can take to improve your financial future.

Not only will proper money-management give you the wherewithal to pursue your dreams, but it is also advantageous to your health. Researchers at Ohio University concluded that individuals with high credit-card debt relative to their income experience more stress-related medical problems than individuals who do not carry such debt. According to RealAge.com, "The more stress people reported that was related to their debt, the more problems they reported with their general health."

So, making the decision to secure your financial position will benefit both your bank account and your physical well-being. The information in this chapter will help you map your path to a sound financial future, simply and effectively.

MAKING YOUR OWN FINANCIAL DECISIONS

If you're accustomed to relying on someone else to make your financial decisions, now is the time to decide to participate in this important arena. Even the most loving, best-intentioned person cannot make the decisions you would make for yourself. It would probably be wise to obtain the services of a good financial advisor, but the final decisions should always be yours.

"Taking charge of one's money has been the 'last frontier' for women," writes Dr. Christopher Hayes of the National Center for Woman and Retirement Research, in the helpful book *Money Makeovers*. Hayes continues:

> Though women have made progress in the workforce and can now be found on almost every rung of the corporate ladder, they often leave their own financial situation on the back burner. During childhood, subliminal messages constantly reinforce the idea that girls aren't supposed to worry about money, and as a result, they are often not exposed to the basic elements of personal finance. . . .

You may have been raised to believe that women simply don't manage money. Nonetheless, the odds are that you not only make many of the decisions about spending your money (or about the family budget), but that you also will have control over more money over time. Many women over forty have expressed the feeling to me that "everything suddenly changed" at some point in their lives. A big part of the "everything" that changed was the need to start managing finances, a task at which their mothers were similarly unskilled. Although managing the household budget has traditionally been the purview of women, investing, earning the primary income, and making the bigger financial decisions have not. In *New Woman* magazine, Jennifer Parris notes:

> While nine out of ten women will be solely responsible for their finances at some point in their lives, few learned much, if anything, about money and investing while they were growing up. And they regret it: 75 percent of adult women wish that someone had encouraged them or taught them about finances when they were young.

Regardless of your age or situation, it is a mistake not to know how your money is being handled. Because the world of savings and investments is quite complex, you may need expert advice. But never abdicate your responsibility to make your own decisions about money. Even if you hold funds jointly with a spouse or other family member, make sure you know how the money is being spent and invested. And make sure that you have a voice in whatever decisions are made. The decisions that affect your future need to be yours.

If you are used to making your own financial decisions, there may still be some aspects of your financial security that you have not considered. You may want to reevaluate your financial plan and make some new decisions about it.

When **Marian's** father died, he was financially unprepared. Because his insurance records were disorganized, he had no will and he left no instructions about the disposal of his estate, Marian was left to sort out the mess for herself and her mother. The process was unnecessarily long, difficult, and costly.

In this one chapter, I cannot set forth a complete financial plan or give specific advice for you as an individual. I will, however, provide a brief overview of budgeting and investments, and give you steps to help you get in control of your financial future. By adhering to the following guidelines, you can assess whether your financial plan is appropriate for your income, your situation, and your desires.

A WOMAN NEEDS A BUDGET

If you read *The 10 Smartest Decisions a Woman Can Make Before 40,* you'll already be familiar with my stand on budgets. Because it's so important for every woman to be in charge of her finances, I'm also including budgeting information here, customized for your life.

Everyone dreads doing a budget, which is why so few actually get done. Although you have been managing money in one form or another for many years, you may still feel somewhat mystified about getting your finances under control. Creating your own budget can make the difference between being financially secure or fiscally confused. You'll find the following steps easy to do and very effective.

Evaluate Your Current Assets

Financial security begins with taking stock of exactly where you stand today. I have taught the following steps to women for many years, with great results. They will give you a start on setting up a budget.

1. WHAT IS YOUR INCOME? Write down the amount of money that comes in monthly. This task is simplest if you (or you and your spouse) have salaries—what you bring home is your income. You may, however, have several sources of income. **Karen's** income includes her basic paycheck as a cashier and the money she makes working overtime. It also includes her additional earnings from her computer business. You might need to include child support, investment income, gifts from family, or other extra revenue. If, like Karen, your earnings vary from month to month, write all your income down for several months to get an average.

2. HOW MUCH DO YOU SPEND? To truly understand how much money you spend, it's important to keep a written record. Write down the following expenditures for a few months until you get to see your average outlay.

   Fixed expenses. Include monthly expenses such as the following: mortgage or rent, utilities (gas, electricity, water, trash pickup), car payment, and other fixed bills. If you are paying off credit card bills, include those payments. Don't forget to note yearly expenses such as property taxes, professional dues and fees, and insurance payments, divided into monthly amounts. Make a list on your computer or in your journal.

   Remaining expenses. Document the rest of your expenditures. One easy way to do this is to pay your bills and your other purchases by check for a few months, and then look back at your check record. Categorize your expenses into clothing, entertainment, groceries, and the like. Don't forget to include debit card payments and ATM withdrawals in your check record. Make a note of the credit card charges that you haven't yet paid. The point is to track all the money you spend. Add this total to your fixed expenses.

Calculate your net income. Subtract your total expenses from your total income. If you have more income than expenses, you're off to a good start. If that allows for savings also, excellent! You don't need more budget help. If your expenses are higher than your income, you need to set up a budget so you won't accumulate debt and create a big problem for yourself.

3. CREATE A SENSIBLE BUDGET. Review your list of fixed expenses. These items will not change quickly, so make sure you have ample income to cover them. If you don't, you'll need to reduce your expenses—move to a less costly apartment, refinance your mortgage for a lower rate, trade in an expensive car for a cheaper one, or pay off debt. Or you can increase your income—negotiate a raise, get a second job or other source of income. If you have more income than you need for fixed expenses, then move on to your discretionary expenses. This is where you have some leeway and where you might be wasting money.

Prioritize your expenses, putting essential items such as food first. Then analyze which expenses you can reduce and set a limit for expenditures on clothing, cosmetics, entertainment, and other discretionary items. Only you can tell which non-essential purchases are most important to you, and which you can cut. Be creative and seek to make as much "profit" as possible in your budget. This net income is your resource for saving, buying property, and investing, as well as traveling and other occasional expenses.

A Money Diet

Sticking to a budget is to your financial health as diet and exercise are to your physical health. If your budget is realistic and based on your actual financial situation (and your personality), as well as your goals, you'll have an easier time adhering to it. Budgets, like health plans, need to be revised as your circumstances change. As you move closer to retirement, it is imperative to incorporate future plans into your budget. Later in this chapter, I'll explore creative moneymaking strategies and ways to tailor your budget over time. Deciding to get into financial shape now can make a huge difference in your future.

In order to survive as a single mother on a cashier's wages, **Karen** needed to take control of her time and money. Through careful budgeting, she was able to stretch her income. She now lives quite comfortably, but she continues to watch her budget. She's saving and investing for her own and her children's future.

If you would like more in-depth information about this topic, I have listed several books in the appendix that can guide you in keeping track of your finances. You can also learn about financial fitness via the Internet and by taking courses at your local community college or other adult education program.

GET APPROPRIATE ADVICE AND INFORMATION

I mentioned earlier that managing your money wisely is not simple. Fortunately, good financial advice is readily available if you know where to look. The following information will help you understand what kinds of advisors are available and where to find them.

Banking Services

People often tell me they feel no connection with the staff at their bank and that bankers cater only to those individuals with sizable accounts. But my experience is different. Where I live, there are smaller, very secure banks with good assets and employees who still believe in providing excellent customer service to loyal clients. Although online banking is convenient, personal interaction is important when you're discussing your financial future. A good banker in a smaller bank or a savings and loan can give you excellent financial information and advice at no cost to you. As I said in *The 10 Smartest Decisions a Woman Can Make Before 40,*

> You're probably in the right bank when you find: a manager who takes the time to talk to you and explain what the bank has to offer for your financial situation; competitive interest rates; the services you want; and a convenient location. Your banker is also a good source for referrals to businesses and professionals in your area.

The staff members at credit unions are also a good resource for advice. If you are eligible to join a credit union through your employer or an association, take advantage of the opportunity. Credit unions are traditionally quite member-oriented and often offer classes on investing and other financial issues, in addition to providing the usual banking services such as checking accounts, low-interest loans, and automatic payroll savings deductions. Some credit unions even offer special group rates on car purchases, vacation packages, and credit cards.

Professional Advisors

A good tax accountant will usually save you more on your taxes than he charges to prepare your return and will advise you in the event of an IRS audit. Some accountants also provide investment services. When selecting a financial advisor, look for one who charges a flat fee for his services. He can give you objective, educated advice on the best investment strategy for you. I would advocate avoiding advisors who earn a commission on the stocks, bonds, annuities, or mutual funds they sell. They may be tempted to put their own interests ahead of yours. Ask friends, family, and colleagues for recommendations and interview prospective advisors until you find one who listens to your goals and treats you with respect. Check the advisor's references and verify his credentials through the resources in the appendix. Your advisor should be willing to have an ongoing dialogue with you about your investment opportunities, changes in your situation, and your financial future.

PLAN FOR A HAPPY SECOND HALF

In *The 10 Smartest Decisions a Woman Can Make Before 40,* I strongly recommended that young women begin planning for a secure financial future. If it's important for younger women, how

135

much more so is it for you? Every woman's financial circumstances are different. By forty, some women have a good start on their financial future, with substantial investment in an Individual Retirement Account or an employer's retirement plan. Some women own a home of their own. Other women find themselves starting over due to a divorce or some financial disaster. Single moms often need every bit of money they earn to keep their family going and don't begin planning for the future until their children are grown. Married or unmarried, women with children who are growing up are facing the huge expense of college.

If you haven't done so, it's time for you to learn everything you can about your finances and take part in making all the decisions concerning your investments.

In my earlier career as an accountant, I taught many classes in financial investing. Whether you're feeling financially secure or starting from scratch, you can benefit from knowing the fundamentals of income management. To give you an idea of your options, an outline of the very basic categories of investment is set forth here.

A word to the wise: don't be fooled by all the media hype about stock options, IPOs, and day-trading. Getting rich quick sounds inviting, but it isn't much more realistic than expecting to win the lottery. Buying and selling stocks on your own is very risky, and it takes a lot of time-consuming research to do so effectively. Fortunes can be lost a good deal more easily than they can be made. There are many other options for generating financial security. Your financial advisor, banker, or seminar instructor can give you more details about investment opportunities that serve your goals.

Savings

The more money you can save, the more you will have to invest. Financial security begins with saving for emergencies, big expenditures (a new roof, a luxury vacation, your child's wedding or education), and for retirement. Whatever your resources are, develop a strategy to save money to attain your financial, career, and life goals. The following guidelines can be used to help you develop or improve your saving habits.

Guidelines for Increasing Your Savings

1. PAY YOURSELF FIRST. This is an old but effective habit. If you put money in savings before you spend it, you'll find it a lot easier to live within your means. "Start by saving 10 percent of your income," suggests Henry S. Brock in *Your Complete Guide to Money Happiness.* "Join your company's 401(k) plan (if you haven't already), or authorize a direct-deposit amount from your checking account into your savings account or a mutual fund every month. Assuming an 8 percent rate of return, your nest egg will double in just nine years."

2. PRACTICE A MONEY DIET. Each time you get a raise, have your additional net earnings deducted and put into savings. Your savings will grow, and you won't miss the extra spending money.

3. SAVE AS THOUGH YOU WERE PAYING A BILL. Using your budget as a guide, decide on an amount you can afford to save each month and write a check on the same day every month, as

though you were paying one of your creditors. Even a small monthly amount will begin to add up.

4. SAVE BEFORE BUYING. If you want an expensive item, such as a new appliance or computer, divide the cost of the item by six, and save that amount every month. Before you know it, you'll have the funds to buy the item without using a high-interest credit card.

5. KEEP MAKING YOUR PREVIOUS PAYMENTS. Once you've finished paying off a car loan or a credit card, continue making the payments on the due date of the original bill—only now *you* are the payee. You won't miss the money because you're not accustomed to having it, and your savings balance will get a great boost.

Saving *before* you spend allows your money to grow rapidly, and it's painless. It's a simple way to guarantee a happy financial future.

Using Credit Wisely

Today, credit cards (or debit cards—on which charges are deducted directly from your checking account) are necessary to rent a car, to order merchandise from a catalog or Web site, and as a reserve for emergencies. But because they are so easy to use, it is very tempting to overspend. For more expensive purchases, seek financing through your bank or credit union and add the fixed monthly payment to your budget. Your goal is to keep your credit cards at zero balances, so they will be available to you in an emergency.

If you faithfully pay your credit card bills in full every month, you won't be charged interest and your statements serve as a record of how you spent the money. You can even keep a record of certain expenses by using one card for a specific reason. For example, if your auto expenses are tax-deductible because you use your car for work, charge all your auto expenses (and nothing else) on one credit card. Those monthly bills, when paid, become a record of these costs for tax purposes. **Karen** got a separate credit card to use for all her home-business expenses, which she paid in full each month. She used the statements at tax time as documentation of deductible expenses for her small computer business.

CREATING A GOOD CREDIT RATING. Your credit rating can be your biggest asset, and at this point in your life you probably have established one. But if you get divorced, are widowed, or have a credit problem, you will need to create a new credit history for yourself.

Start to develop a good credit rating with the bills you're already paying. Make sure that your phone or utility company is crediting you (rather than your ex) for the timely payments. Then, use these companies as references on credit applications. Buy some small item on credit at a store that offers credit readily and pay it off on time (which will cost you a small amount of interest). You can then add that store to your list of references. Apply for a credit card through your bank or credit union, using your savings for collateral if necessary. If you and your spouse had joint credit cards, obtain one in your own name with a separate bill.

Sally married soon after college. She and her husband owned a house and had joint investments. When they divorced ten years later, the proceedings were expensive, and they had to sell the house to split the proceeds. Sally had to reestablish credit in her own name. She began through her credit union at work, where she had always had an account. The credit union issued her a credit card that she used and paid off every month, just to create credit. Once she had a satisfactory record, it was easy to get other cards.

Basic Investments

There are a vast number of ways you can invest your money, and new investment opportunities are always arising. Unless you are *very* savvy about the advantages and disadvantages of a particular investment, it is a good idea to discuss it with a professional before you go forward. In this section, I'll describe the most common types of investments to give you a basic understanding of the variety that is available. Unless you want to dedicate a significant portion of your life to learning about the stock market, it's a good idea to stick to more basic, time-honored investments such as real estate, employer stock options, mutual funds, bonds, annuities, retirement plans, and IRAs.

Ruth and her husband have substantial investments, with the majority of them in his corporate retirement account. He has his retirement well provided for. Ruth, however, has always saved a little of the money she earned working, just to have some funds at her own discretion. She invested some of these savings at the advice of an uncle who is a financial planner and is planning to use another portion to set up a business for herself.

Recently, **Sally's** major investment has been in her consulting business. Because she had accrued substantial savings from her years as an executive, she had the security she needed to venture forth into consulting work.

OWN YOUR OWN HOME. Consider purchasing a home if you don't already own one. Unless you live in an affluent urban area, it is usually possible to buy your own home at a reasonable price, and most investment counselors recommend that you do. Many state programs and the federal government offer purchasing incentives to "first-time buyers" and women. Through these programs, you can buy a home with a small down payment. If you look in smaller communities or surrounding neighborhoods, you can often find excellent values and move to an even more desirable home later when your house or condo increases in value.

There are many seminars and books available on buying property. Make sure your real-estate agent or broker is highly recommended by friends, family, or your financial advisor or banker. A good real-estate agent should be able to guide you in the following: the risks and benefits of owning your own home, references to reliable lenders, escrow companies and title researchers, zoning laws and the desirability of a property's location, and special programs for new homeowners.

Check with your local real-estate licensing board to ensure that your agent or broker is properly licensed and that he or she has a good professional record. Ask to talk to previous clients and find out if they're happy with the agent's services. Have any purchase carefully appraised and compared to the other properties surrounding it before you decide whether the price is acceptable. If you buy at a relatively low price and plan to keep the house for the long term, the odds are your house will increase in value over a number of years.

Obviously, you'll want to make sure you can afford your loan payment. You can (very roughly) estimate that a mortgage payment will be about 1 percent of the amount you pay for a house or condominium. For example, if the property costs $100,000, you can roughly estimate a mortgage payment of about $1,000 per month. If you buy in a price range you can comfortably afford now, you'll be able to enjoy your new house and not feel overly stressed.

In addition to the amount of money you'll spend on the actual purchase, you should factor in the amount of time and money it will take to maintain the property. If you have experience with yardwork or gardening and enjoy doing it, then a house with a yard won't be too overwhelming. And keep in mind that an older house can require frequent expenditures for plumbing, electrical wiring, and painting. If you are unwilling to invest in repairs and upkeep, you may want to purchase a condo or a townhouse where most of these responsibilities are assumed by the owners' association. You'll need to participate in the condo association so you'll have a voice in decisions that will affect your property. Owning a house or condo is not like renting; there's no landlord to call, and you must manage all the problems yourself. On the other hand, you do get to make (or participate in) the decisions about repairs and renovations.

Because mortgage payments are tax-deductible for most people and you can generally make a profit when selling a home, it's a good investment for almost everyone.

INCOME PROPERTY. Many older women and couples find that owning rentals is an excellent source of extra income. Once the mortgage is paid off, most of the rent becomes profit. But be aware that managing rental property is work. You will have to collect the rent, maintain the accounting records, deal with troublesome tenants, make any necessary repairs, and keep the property in good condition. If the rental income is sufficient, you may be able to hire a property-management company to fill vacancies, collect rents, and contract for repairs and maintenance. The agency will regularly report to you about the status of your property and will contact you if a special repair or expense arises. If you find a reputable, reliable management agency for a reasonable fee, this is the easiest way to look after a property, especially if you don't live near it. If you do decide to manage the building yourself, contact your local Apartment Owners' Association, a non-profit group with offices in most cities. The group's purpose is to enable landlords to get together and share information, work with the city council on zoning and other laws affecting property owners, and educate owners about the legal aspects of rentals.

STOCKS—TODAY'S GLAMOUR INVESTMENT. With all the media attention on the stock market today, the only worthwhile investments seem to involve buying stocks. If you want to spend the time and effort learning about the very complicated and volatile market, you can indeed do well investing for yourself—but you must be aware of the risks. Take classes or read books (see the appendix) to educate yourself about the pros and cons of playing the market.

As an alternative to investing on your own, you can join an investment club. These are groups of private investors who meet on a regular basis to learn about the market, research stocks, and pool their money for investing. The National Association of Investors Corporation (NAIC) offers educational products and start-up information to individuals who want to start or join investment clubs. When investing in the stock market, the NAIC encourages people to follow these four principles: invest a set amount regularly once a month, regardless of market conditions; reinvest dividends and capital gains; buy growth stocks; and diversify your portfolio. If you don't have the time and motivation to learn all about the stock market, you will need to consult a professional. Your investment counselor may be licensed to help you or may refer you to a licensed broker.

MUTUAL FUNDS. For the more cautious investor, mutual funds may be more appealing. Mutual funds are designed for the investor who doesn't have the time, information, or motivation to follow the market closely enough to choose stocks. They are a smart choice if you want to invest only a few thousand dollars at once or for the investment of small amounts on a monthly or quarterly basis. Mutual funds provide the benefit of diversification, without having to invest a lot of money in a huge portfolio. Investing small amounts in a mutual fund is a great way to get started in the stock market, with less risk and less work than investing for yourself.

A good fund manager will minimize risk and maximize profit, but how can you tell which funds are reliable? Again, research or good advice from your counselor or broker will help.

ANNUITIES AND BONDS. Annuities are a retirement insurance policy. In return for paying monthly premiums now, you are guaranteed income at retirement age. Our parents' generation invested heavily in annuities, but they are less popular today, because other types of investments usually provide a better rate of return. Annuities are usually sold by commissioned salesmen who may not be able to give you impartial advice, so double-check the wisdom of purchasing any annuity with your investment counselor.

Bonds are shares in government loans (as a bond investor you are loaning money to the government). They are initiated by governments to raise funds and are often tax-free. Many countries issue bonds, which are rated according to safety and return on investment. You probably have seen U.S. Government Savings Bonds, which mature (attain their full value) in a certain number of years but don't pay a high rate of interest. You may have bought some for your children or grandchildren. Other kinds of bonds (municipal bonds, Canadian government bonds) give you a much better return, however, and many are tax-free or tax-deferred, so consider these when consulting with your financial advisor.

STOCK OPTIONS AND RETIREMENT FUNDS. If your employer has a retirement plan, the plan's funds are usually invested in stocks. Many company retirement plans are an excellent value. If your company has a plan in which it matches your contribution with company funds, it is usually a great opportunity to increase your investment rapidly. If you have invested in a company plan for a number of years, it's important that you know how your plan works. Your employer is required to explain your retirement plan options, and you should take advantage of any seminars or written materials it provides. Usually a member of the Human Resources department can assist you. When you understand the offerings of your company's plan, discuss them with your financial advisor.

Be aware, however, that you may forgo getting fully vested in a corporate retirement plan by changing jobs. If you expect to move from company to company, as many people do these days, you may be better off investing in an IRA (discussed following).

Many large employers such as Home Depot, General Electric, Microsoft, and Amazon.com offer their employees stock-option plans. These plans permit staff members to invest a limited amount of their earnings in corporate stock, often in conjunction with the company retirement plan. In some situations a company will match the employee's investment in the corporate stock, up to a limit. If you have such a plan available to you, explore this investment option with your adviser.

Karen, who lived on a very tight budget and spent every cent she took home from her job at the grocery store, made sure she contributed the maximum allowed to her union retirement account. Every time she received a raise, she put the net increase into her retirement. "That way," she explains, "I didn't have to try and deny myself or the children something so I could save. We had whatever I brought home, and I made it go as far as it could; if I came up with a little extra, we could splurge on something, and I knew my future was secure."

INDIVIDUAL RETIREMENT ACCOUNTS. Individual Retirement Accounts (IRAs) are accounts you can invest in, without having to pay taxes on the income until you withdraw the funds at retirement (when you're in a lower tax bracket). There are several different types of individual retirement accounts, including accounts for self-employed individuals. The laws regulating IRAs change from time to time, and your banker or financial counselor can help you decide what kind of account is right for you.

Sally had an IRA through her employer's retirement plan, which she converted to a SEP-IRA (Self-Employed Individual Retirement Account) when she began her consulting business. She contributes on a monthly basis, according to her income that month, even beyond the maximum allowed for tax deduction. "I know I have no benefits except those I supply for myself," she says, "I need to think about my future now."

By considering all your financial options carefully, you can set up an appropriate and secure financial future for yourself.

ESTATE PLANNING

If you have successfully invested your income, own valuable property, or have life insurance, estate planning is vital. An estate plan will serve to preserve the value of the estate for your heirs, ease the complications of probate, and reduce inheritance taxes. Estate planning is not just writing a will to distribute your assets when you pass away. The plan can include: gifts to your heirs during your lifetime; a trust that is managed by you until your death and managed by designated trustees afterward; distributing your assets into IRAs and other retirement accounts to minimize tax liability; and a living will or a durable power of attorney.

A good financial lawyer or estate planner can help you decide which aspects of an estate plan are appropriate for your situation and can draft the legal documents to effect your wishes.

Marian's father died intestate (without a will), which created great difficulties for her mother. Marian understood that her father had not wanted to think about his own death or pay a lawyer to write a will, but she was determined to learn from her father's example. She and her mother signed a durable power of attorney for health care (known also as a living will). With proper legal advice, they also set up a trust (which included a will) for the remainder of her mother's estate. The trust would be jointly administered by both of them while her mother was alive and would then pass to Marian, as her mother wished, without a severe tax penalty for Marian.

Wills

In my counseling practice, I see time and again how important wills are to family happiness. You have a responsibility to your heirs to clearly state your wishes. It's a difficult topic, but not discussing what will happen in the event of your death is asking for your loved ones to be hurt, bewildered, and perhaps even struggle bitterly with each other. If you don't want to create that kind of scenario, you'll make plans in advance and let your family know what your wishes are. To draw a proper will, it is wise to consult an attorney.

Durable Power of Attorney for Health Care (Living Will)

A living will is a document in which you designate someone to make health-care decisions should you become unable to do so. It is essential to plan for your own care should you become ill. A durable power of attorney for health care (also known as a living will) is a statement of your health-care wishes and relieves your family from having to make difficult choices for you. In this document, you can note whether you want to be given life support, to donate organs, and who has the right to make decisions about your health care and even the care of your body after you die.

To make certain that your living will is enforceable, it must be executed in compliance with the laws of your state. Generally, a living will should be signed before witnesses and notarized. At many hospitals a staff member will ask you to execute a living will if you are having surgery or have a serious illness, as it is much easier for the staff to follow a written directive from you rather than the various opinions of your family. If you have a living will, inform your family of where it is kept and bring it with you whenever you are admitted to a hospital.

Living Trusts

If you have considerable assets, or if you have some concern about who will inherit your property (for example, if you have children from more than one marriage), you may derive peace of mind by creating a living trust. Basically, a living trust holds your assets in the name of the trust that you, as trustee, control while you're alive and which a designated trustee (of your choice) will manage after your death. The tax advantages of living trusts (determined by the laws of your state and federal law) are usually very beneficial, avoiding probate and most inheritance taxes. Living trusts are extremely flexible, giving you many options of how to dispose of your estate. For example, you may leave part of your estate to charity, while retaining part of it to be given to your children when they come of age.

Ruth's oldest daughter has had marital problems and is now pregnant. To ensure the security of their first grandchild, Ruth and Paul have created a living trust, with their grandchild as beneficiary. In the event both Ruth and Paul die, a bank will act as trustee of the assets. This gives them confidence that their grandchild will be adequately provided for, no matter what the parents do.

If you create a living trust, in most states it will contain both a will and a durable power of attorney for health care, because these documents are considered so important.

If you make estate planning an integral part of your retirement plan, you'll be assured that your future is secure and that you have done your best to provide for your beneficiaries' security as well.

PARTNERSHIP AGREEMENTS AND PROMISSORY NOTES

If you decide to engage in a business with someone, to purchase property, or share investments with someone other than your spouse, you might want to have a partnership agreement. Before marriage, many adults who own separate property also sign prenuptial agreements (which is a type of partnership agreement).

A partnership agreement is a legal document, usually drawn by a lawyer and registered in the court, that spells out the rights and responsibilities of all partners to any agreement involving money, property, or the possibility of future profits. The agreement sets forth what happens if one partner dies, if the partnership is dissolved, and how the profits of the partnership are to be distributed. It can also cover other agreements, such as financial reports and tax liabilities. Such agreements are invaluable and you should never enter into a financial arrangement with *anyone,* no matter how close you are, without one. Keep in mind that if your partner passes away, the executors of his or her estate could have the right to make decisions affecting your finances.

The importance of a partnership agreement was brought home to me personally when I wrote *The 10 Smartest Decisions a Woman Can Make Before 40.* My friend and colleague, Elizabeth Friar Williams, who had begun a book proposal with this title, had become ill. Our mutual agent, Laurie Harper, asked if I would help finish the proposal and share in writing the book, because Betsy was not well enough to do it. When I agreed, Laurie drew up a clear partnership agreement. Contrary to our expectations, Betsy suddenly died. Because of the agreement, it was still possible to sell the book to a publisher, and my rights and the rights of Betsy's estate were very clear. Because all rights reverted to me after Betsy's death, the agreement also made it possible for me to write this book. I was honored to carry on with the first book in Betsy's name as well as my own, and I'm grateful that all the rights were protected and I was free to follow up with this book.

SHORT OF CASH? GET CREATIVE!

If you're anticipating your retirement and you fear that you have started planning and saving too late in the day, it's time to get creative. You may want to start a small business in addition to your primary job or learn how to make the most of your investments. Perhaps this would be a good time to take advantage of a talent (such as writing, or musical or artistic abilities) or a business skill (such as child care, consulting, or teaching). Any of these can be a great way to increase your income while having a good time. Many adults create "mini-jobs" to supplement their retirement income.

From the time she began her computer training, **Karen** supplemented her income with extra work. At school she would tutor other students with their computer assignments. Later, she would spend nights designing Web pages at home or helping friends with their software problems. With close friends, Karen exchanged child care, cooking, carpentry, or other skills for her computer expertise. She charged a reasonable fee to others. Over time, this work brought her a significant amount of extra income.

No matter what your income or financial situation, if you begin to budget, plan, save, and invest, you can create the secure future you want. The earlier you begin, of course, the more security you can create.

CHAPTER 7

Never Too Late:
Decide to Be the Person You
Might Have Been

*While others may argue about whether the world ends with a bang
or a whimper, I just want to make sure mine doesn't end with a whine.*
—Barbara Gordon

Midlife is a time to focus on the deeper issues—your dreams and goals, and your emotional and spiritual development. The years after forty gradually become more about meaning and satisfaction and less about obligations and accomplishments. As you mature, you can focus on living the life you always wanted to live, tempered by the wisdom you have gained through your experiences. Up to this point, your life may have been centered around other peoples' wants and the demands of work, home, and family, and although those responsibilities continue, this is the time to bring your personal dreams into reality. Time and again, I find that the women I counsel are happier with other aspects of their lives when they are happier with themselves. It's time to live your life to the fullest. It's time to decide what you want to do for yourself.

WHEN YOU GROW UP

You have learned many things about yourself throughout your life. You know how you deal with success, work, financial decisions, family, friends, and your other relationships. But how much attention have you paid to your relationship with yourself? To make your dreams come true, you must turn within to discover what will make you happy. "[T]he reality of life is that the quality of life does not depend directly on what others think of us or on what we own," writes University of Chicago researcher Mihaly Csikszentmihalyi in *Flow: The Psychology of Optimal Experience.* "The bottom line is, rather, how we feel about ourselves and about what happens to us. To improve life one must improve the quality of experience."

In chapter 4, you explored your friendship style with others, and your internal friendship as well. How well have you done at developing this friendship with yourself? In this chapter, you'll use that internal friendship as a basis for the changes you want to make in your life. You have an opportunity now to re-create yourself, to be and do all the things you've always dreamed of.

Guidelines for Building on Your Inner Friendship

The following guidelines will help you further develop your internal relationship and apply what you've learned to your daily life.

I. ASK YOUR OWN OPINION. Now that you have a model for internal friendship, develop it through practice. About five times a day ask yourself: "What do I think about this? Do I like it?

Does it make sense to me? Do I agree or disagree with the others? If I had unlimited power, what would I do?" By doing this, you'll get used to asking your own opinion of ideas and events.

2. LISTEN TO YOUR ANSWERS. Listen to your opinions as you would to the ideas of a respected friend. Consider them, weigh them, and even discuss them with yourself from time to time. Allow them to influence your daily thoughts. If you feel, for example, that your work does not give you enough satisfaction, just accept that feeling. Eventually it will create a need to act and give you many exciting ideas for how to act. You needn't act on your ideas right away. At first, just practice listening to your answers. After a few weeks of practice, you will have easy access to your own ideas and feelings. Let your ideas incubate at their own pace. Over time, an awareness of your own opinion will have a profound but gradual effect on what you do and how you behave.

3. SPEND TIME WITH YOURSELF. Using these tools for communicating with yourself, spend some time alone, every day if possible, considering what you would like to change about your life. If your schedule is very busy, use the time in the shower, driving to work, or while doing simple chores to examine what you would like to change about yourself and your life. Look back in your journal to the roles you chose in the "New Life Evaluation" exercise (see page 65) from chapter 2 and compare them to the life you would like to have. Explore your dreams and fantasies to see if there are any you want to accomplish now.

As a working mom, **Marian** had very little time for herself, and whatever time she did have seemed to just disappear. She decided to dedicate her commute to and from work to thinking about herself and her future. She got a voice-activated tape recorder, so she could record memos as she got ideas. She turned the radio and her cell phone off while she was in the car and spent the time focusing on driving and making plans.

If devoting time to your own inner friendship sounds selfish to you, think again. When your internal-interaction skills are strong, you develop a solid internal role model on which to base your relationships with others. Ultimately, both you and your loved ones benefit.

DISCOVER YOUR DREAMS

In my counseling office, I have several colorful illustrations by the very talented Jodie Bergsma. These fanciful depictions of elves, fairies, animals, and children create a gentle, pleasant, storybook atmosphere. The motto on one of them is, "It's never too late to be who you might have been." Every day, in therapy, clients discover this truth. As they explore within, they discover old dreams and new ones, which, once known, can become a new reality.

If you allow yourself to dream, to aspire, you will begin to plan—and once you have a plan, you can begin taking steps to make it real. Using our limited time on the planet for a purpose— to create something that is unique, special, and feels good to us and is both exciting and satisfying. Revered philosopher-professor Dr. Joseph Campbell, author of *The Power of Myth,* advised us to "follow our bliss." He believed that when people are energized by their dreams, they can save the world by bringing their own truth and energy to it.

According to author and researcher Marsha Sinetar, there is a "predictable sequence" to the "life-enhancing choices" made by people who transform their lives. In her book *Elegant Choices, Healing Choices,* she outlines the steps of the experience of becoming your true self.

- We choose in a wholesome direction *despite* feelings of fear or our need to cling to the familiar.

- Instead of avoiding those things we fear, we start pro-actively selecting those ways of being, thinking, and acting that most efficiently take us toward what we consciously want.

- Our self-acceptance for our truest, "living self" increases . . . we move to present our real self to others, to live our real selves in our lives.

- Ultimately, our choices *flow* from this core-self, instead of being *forced*. . . . We are faithfully courageous and loving toward ourselves and—eventually—toward others. . . . Growing more closely attuned to our inner workings, we also grow more conscious and self-accepting.

- Soon we notice how our negative feelings can actually *help* us and provide information to us much as a mirror or photograph.

When people allow their dreams to be important, their lives take on more meaning, they feel better about themselves, and their energy and enthusiasm rise. "Growing more closely attuned to our inner workings, we also grow more conscious and self-accepting." writes Sinetar in *Ordinary People as Monks and Mystics*.

Whether you've always wanted to heal the planet or just have time to walk in the woods, this is the time for you to do it. Midlife is that exquisite time when you realize that you don't have all the time left in the world, and you need to take advantage of your energy, wisdom, enthusiasm, and vitality while you still have them. Perhaps you want to learn to live more simply or become politically active. Whatever your dream, simple or complex, if you allow it to emerge, you can find the strength and skills to actualize it.

WHO ARE YOU REALLY?

As a child in Sunday school, you may have been taught: "What I am is God's gift to me, what I become is my gift to God." Think of yourself and your life as a gift you are giving. As a result of your life experience, you have become a marvelous package of talents and skills—these talents and skills are your gift. The skills you already possess may be enough to actualize your dream and make the changes you want to make. Learning to think positively about who you are, and therefore to make the best of each of your traits and talents, will enable you to operate at your most powerful and to be truly satisfied with the results.

You may have always thought you were too quiet or too talkative, too aggressive or too passive; but what happens if you recast "too quiet" to mean that you're a good listener or "too talkative" to mean you are an excellent communicator? Traits you perceive as being too aggressive can be considered leadership qualities, and "too passive" traits can mean you're an excellent supporter or follow-up person. When you think of personality traits as distinct colors in a palette, you realize that each of the colors can be useful in the right circumstance—so how do you discover the colors of your own personal palette?

Many techniques have been suggested to help people who want to get in touch with the many different aspects of their personality, including hypnosis, writing with the non-dominant hand, journaling, and various internal dialogues—all of which are helpful. One of the simplest tools you can use is your mirror. Mirrors provide an easy way to become aware of yourself and to learn how to use your various characteristics to maximize your success and happiness. "Mirror work is very powerful," writes Louise Hay in *You Can Heal Your Life*. "To look yourself straight in the eye and make a positive declaration about yourself is, in my opinion, the quickest way to get results."

"To cultivate a friendship with myself I find that I need to take time each day to sit with myself" writes Carol Putnam in an *In Context* article titled "My Selves in the Mirror." "I can observe, direct and harmonize my mental, physical and emotional processes . . . I can welcome home all the parts of me that I exiled long ago."

Mirror Dialogue

To add mirror work to the previous exercise, follow these steps:

I. TALK TO A MIRROR. Set aside some private time and look into a small mirror. Greet yourself as you would a friend. Take some time to get comfortable with yourself.

2. BE YOUR OWN FRIEND. Share with yourself your feelings, your hopes, and your dreams for today and the future. Tell yourself at least three things you like about yourself, and remind yourself of your skills, talents, and abilities. Respond to these compliments and acknowledgments, and listen to your response. If you do this for a few minutes, you may find that you are expressing two different points of view about something, usually pro and con. Perhaps you have dreams and wishes that seem to be in conflict, or you may have negative reactions to your hopes.

Julie's conflict about taking care of her parents really emerged when she spoke with herself in the mirror. She felt as if one inner voice wanted to run away, and the other worried about whether she could care for her parents well enough.

As you get more comfortable, you'll find you can have discussions about problems and issues you are facing. Talking over all the aspects of the situation with yourself will help alleviate your confusion, especially whenever you are undecided or "of two minds" about a decision.

Julie found that letting each of the conflicting voices "tell its story" helped her clarify issues she faced and made decisions clearer.

3. RESOLVE ISSUES. Work with your different points of view until you resolve them into a more inclusive viewpoint. By doing this exercise several times, you will become more comfortable with facing yourself, your strengths and weaknesses, and when you become aware of an "internal argument" and divided opinions, you'll know how to reach an agreeable solution.

Each time you repeat these steps, you will have an easier time identifying and understanding your inner thinking and clearing up your confusion. Soon you will be able to "negotiate" internal problems very quickly, think more clearly, and make decisions with much less struggle.

Daily Review

You can use the internal communication tools you learn in the mirror exercise to become aware of your deepest wishes and desires, and to clear up problems on a daily basis. You can use the following additional steps to support yourself as you make the changes you desire in your life.

1. SET ASIDE TIME FOR REVIEW. At the end of the day, set aside some quiet time for a review and discussion with yourself. You can do this in a bubble bath, shower, or hot tub, in your snug bed, on your sofa with a soothing cup of herbal tea, or during a walk, a jog, or a yoga session if you wish. If your time is limited, you can even do it while driving, riding public transportation, or waiting in line. If your family is watching TV, you can take a few minutes in another room to do your review.

2. REVIEW YOUR DAY. Review the significant events of your day in reverse order (that is, the most recent event first, working back to the morning).

3. EVALUATE AND PRAISE. Keeping a positive, supportive attitude toward yourself, evaluate each of your interactions and choices, and praise yourself for what you did well.

4. REPLAY YOUR MISTAKES. If you had interactions you did not like, or made choices you feel were wrong, "replay" the scene in your memory, doing it over and over as if it were a video. In your replays, change your behavior and responses until you are satisfied with the outcome. You can also replay conversations that didn't go as well as you would have liked by "playing the tape" of the conversation from your memory, trying different responses, "rewinding" the memory tape, and trying it again. You can replay it as many times as you need, until it comes out the way you want it to. This is a way to experiment with new behaviors while you discover new options and reactions to people and events, and to create new, more effective choices.

When **Marian** decided to apply for a full-time position at law firms, she hadn't had a job interview for some time. For her first two interviews, she chose less desirable positions as practice, and she was indeed nervous—as she had feared she would be. Later, at home, she "replayed" the interviews, trying new answers to each question she had been asked until she felt more confident about her performance. In this way she got to "practice" interviewing. At subsequent interviews, Marian was poised, sharp, and performed quite well.

5. PLAN TO GET NEEDED INFORMATION. If you find that to have more satisfying interactions or to make better choices you need skills or information that you do not have, you can do some research or get some coaching. Write a note to yourself about the information you need. ("I need to know proper introductions—get etiquette book from library" or "How should I

respond to Harry when he tries to make me feel guilty? Discuss with Sue—she seems to manage this situation well.") Make sure you have whatever you need to feel confident that you can gracefully incorporate new skills into your everyday behavior.

6. REVIEW YOUR ENVIRONMENT AND INTERACTIONS. Evaluate how others related to you. Notice who was supportive and caring. Plan to have more contact with those who back you and your dreams and to let them know you appreciate them. For people who were not supportive, practice confronting them, approaching them differently, or making a specific request to be treated in a certain way. Visualize doing this until you feel confident.

7. RECAP AND THANK YOURSELF. When you've reviewed the significant events in your day, praise yourself for the things well done and conclude the session. You'll find if you do this simple review every day for three weeks, it will become second nature, and you'll also be able to do a mini-version of it no matter where you are. With this easy, effective system you'll be able to keep track of your progress toward making your dreams come true. Record your discoveries in your journal.

GETTING MOTIVATED

I mentioned earlier that making changes is hard work. You can know yourself very well and know what you want to do, but you still need to know how to get motivated. How do you keep your energy up for the changes you want to make?

When you were younger, you may have learned to keep yourself going with negative methods—that is, either by threatening yourself ("If I don't get this done, I'll be fired"); beating yourself up ("You lazy thing, you get out of bed"); or by scaring yourself ("You'd better work hard or no one will like you"). Perhaps, like many women, you've gotten your motivation by doing things for others. By this time in life, however, the people you've been focused on may no longer need you as much as before, and you've probably discovered that negative reinforcement is a very poor motivator. Both methods of motivation usually lead to burnout and emotional exhaustion, even depression.

If you find it difficult to remain excited by your goal or to follow through on changes, try a new approach.

CELEBRATION AND MOTIVATION

For many years I've been successfully teaching my clients to motivate themselves with a simple equation:

$$\text{celebration} + \text{appreciation} = \text{motivation}$$

Because you are in charge of your own life, you have a choice about how you want to treat yourself. To keep yourself motivated, treat yourself with kindness and understanding; be generous with praise and gentle with corrections. You will feel energized and will accomplish your goals with a sense of pride in your achievement and a great deal of pleasure. You'll wonder why you never realized how easy it was. This can be accomplished through the two "magic motivators": celebration and appreciation. Most of us know how to appreciate others. When it comes to ourselves, however, we feel embarrassed and uncomfortable if we are too generous with praise.

Years of being told not to brag or be cocky when we were young have taken their toll, and self-appreciation comes awkwardly. If motivation is a desirable trait, however, self-appreciation becomes necessary and desirable too. The good news is that you can learn how to effectively (and appropriately) appreciate who you are.

Guidelines for Motivation Through Celebration

To create motivation to follow through on your dreams, try the following ideas.

1. CREATE A PICTURE OF YOUR DREAM. Using pictures cut from magazines or your own artwork, create a collage or picture of what your dream will look like. Place a photo of yourself in the picture to represent the fulfillment of your desire.

2. WRITE DOWN ALL THE ADVANTAGES OF ACHIEVING YOUR GOAL. When you become the woman you have always wanted to be, whether you're making a big change or a small one, what will the benefits be?

3. WHAT KIND OF PEOPLE AND EXPERIENCES WILL YOUR NEW DREAM BRING INTO YOUR LIFE? Imagining all the new events and connections you'll experience will raise your enthusiasm.

4. NOTICE EVERY SMALL SUCCESS ON THE WAY TO ACHIEVING YOUR DREAM. Each time you notice, celebrate, and appreciate your accomplishments, you generate energy to take the next step.

The more creative your celebrations are, and the more fun they are, the more energy you'll generate.

5. KEEP YOUR DREAM A SECRET UNTIL IT FEELS SOLID. Be careful about who you share your dream with until you feel strong enough to resist the negative influence of others who may unknowingly discourage you. Keeping a dream secret makes it more special and increases your energy for it.

6. SHOW YOUR GRATITUDE. If you dream of good friendships or a great marriage, learn to celebrate the joys of your relationship. If you have a partner, make a point of expressing your appreciation and gratitude on a daily basis. You'll soon find your behavior is reciprocated. Even with a long-term friend or partner, remember to do some of the little things you probably did early in your relationship. The gift of a single flower or a card, a special food, or even just a squeeze of the hand and a smile can energize your relationship or friendship. Taking time to care about what's important to the other person, and to listen, means a lot.

Controlling Outside Influences

If friends or family react negatively to your plans, criticize you, or advise you in an unhelpful manner, you'll notice that your energy begins to drain away. Until your plans are strong and actually working, and you can point to some success, share them only with people you know will be supportive in a helpful way. Don't ask for comments from people who tend to be critical, and if you get unsolicited criticism deflect it by cutting the conversation short and debriefing yourself afterward. Sharing your dream with people who will support what you are doing is a great way to keep yourself motivated.

Information from books, articles, television, and the Internet can also help you stay motivated—but be selective in your research. Take only what you find helpful, and don't assume that the source of information knows more than you do about your dream. Don't ever accept such information at face value. If you come across "facts" that are discouraging, argue with them. Find ways around them. Think critically about what is being presented, choose the ideas that are helpful to you, and reject any that drain your motivation.

Remember, every person who ever created something new was doing something that "couldn't be done." Celebrate and appreciate the wisdom of your own life. If your energy is low and your enthusiasm is beginning to fade, make sure you are celebrating and appreciating who you are and what you have already accomplished. Use mirror work, the daily review, and the guidelines for celebrating your dream to reenergize yourself.

Celebrating the Little Things

We're accustomed to celebrating "major" events, such as graduating from school, but why wait for a big occasion to recognize your achievements? What about getting a good grade in chemistry? By celebrating that the glass is "half full," rather than focusing on everything that isn't just perfect, you'll keep a better perspective on your accomplishments. And by making a fuss over every small step along the way, you'll feel that you've accomplished more.

As a young single mom, **Karen** faced an overwhelming future, but the people in her church helped her stay focused by giving her lots of encouragement and emotional support. Every week they would find something to celebrate. Each time her children passed a school test, and each time Karen learned something new at work, the whole congregation congratulated her and wished her well. These celebrations kept her spirits up and reminded her to focus on what she had accomplished rather than on how far she still had to go. Now that she is very successful at her work, creating a computer business at home and trying out a singing career, her church members are cheering her on. Karen stops to pray and give thanks often for all the help she has received along the way.

Soothing, Reassuring, and Relaxing Yourself

When was the last time you really pampered yourself? A little relaxation will go far to keep you motivated to move toward the new you. Develop a style for recharging and relaxing. What makes you most comfortable? What soothes you? What helps you feel reenergized? Make a list of your favorite "personal rechargers." Your list might include taking a bubble bath, doing yoga, listening to your favorite music, taking a long walk in the country, enjoying a phone conversation with your best friend, or taking a nap. Make sure the list includes simple things you can do at no cost (such as relaxing with a cup of tea and reading a favorite book) and things that are very special (such as spending a day at a bed-and-breakfast or having a massage and a facial). Keep the list where you can refer to it whenever you feel the need to recharge, and make use of it often.

With the stress she was under, **Julie** knew she needed to recharge regularly. She developed a list of things to do, divided into categories. Free: walk on the beach; read a favorite book; listen to music; take a nap. Low cost: bring takeout food home; buy a magazine and read it in bed; rent a video; buy a new color of lipstick or nail polish. Higher cost: have dinner with friends at a nice restaurant; get a massage; hire nursing help for a day. She kept adding to her lists, and when she felt the need to recharge, she'd just pull out the lists and choose something to do. She showed her lists to a few friends and found that they'd surprise her periodically with one of the things on her list—they'd invite her to dinner, or drop by with a book, CD, or video for her to enjoy.

MAKING YOUR DREAMS A REALITY

By using these tools, you can implement all of your decisions and make your dreams come true. There's really nothing scary about making changes in your life. When you think about it, you're changing every day; your experiences and interactions contribute to your daily (sometimes imperceptible) growth.

Make the exercises in this chapter part of your daily life—you will bring a heightened awareness to your growing abilities and know-how, and continue to use what you know about yourself to set your priorities. Through appreciation and celebration, you can keep yourself continually motivated, gently yet effectively, until you bring your dreams into your reality.

CHAPTER 8

Lighten Up:
Decide to Have More Fun

Taking joy in life is a woman's best cosmetic.
—Rosalind Russell

L ife is not supposed to be all seriousness—to really feel that life is worth living, we need to have some fun. Yes, *fun.* You remember fun! Pleasure, humor, leisure activities, and silliness are ways we recharge, renew our energy, restore our hope and positive outlook, and connect with others. Fun creates a deep internal connection too; through play we reconnect with our hearts, our childlike selves, and the intuitive, spontaneous part of our psyches.

For many people today, the definition of "fun" has become distorted. Some people's ideas of what is fun are connected with excess, such as having a couple of drinks or engaging in "extreme" sports. Some people think that to have fun, they must spend a lot of money traveling or dining out. Others think that they must be around the "right kind of people." Saddest of all are those who rely on others to "create" their fun.

171

Fun does not depend on spending money or going to extremes. It does not depend on a particular setting, companion, or activity. Having fun is an internal process. You can have fun sitting still and thinking about interesting or enjoyable things, or working in your garden, petting the cat, talking quietly with a friend, or playing cards. Singing, dancing, playing a sport, and drawing are fun pastimes for some people. I've even met women who like to solve math problems for fun!

"Most of us equate choosing fun with irresponsibility, selfishness, and immaturity . . . believing that fun . . . is incompatible with the deep commitment, profound trust, and close spiritual bond we also want," writes journalist Dalma Heyn in "Why Girls Don't Wanna Have Fun," *New Woman*, June 1995. "Fun is sexy. It's life-affirming. It's subversive. . . . Fun turns *into* trust; fun *creates* respect; fun *produces* a spiritual bond; fun *generates* intimacy. Seen this way, as a catalyst rather than an afterthought, fun is hardly trivial."

EVERYDAY FUN

Many of us think of fun as something we do on special occasions, something that requires a bit of advance planning. We have whole industries dedicated to helping us play—it seems as though a new theme park opens every week. When you look back on your most joyous life experiences, however, they are more likely to have been spontaneous and simple rather than elaborate and expensive. Play is recreation—activity that "re-creates" and causes you to see life differently and be refreshed by the change.

You don't have to separate play and fun from anything else you're doing. A lighthearted approach to serious matters often is the most productive one.

You already know what is fun to you. Go back and review your responses to "Guidelines for Motivation Through Celebration" (see page 165) in the last chapter. Your personal keys to fun and play are right there. I'm sure you can recall a time when you tried so hard to create some fun that you actually prevented it from happening. "When you discard arrogance, complexity, and a few other things that get in the way," writes Benjamin Hoff in *The Tao of Pooh,* "sooner or later you will discover that simple, childlike and mysterious secret . . . Life is Fun."

Fun is a creative and spiritual experience. It is simply an expression of your delight in life's everyday occurrences. In the midst of work, you can play. It takes only a change of focus to turn a serious moment into fun. A wink, a smile, and a shared laugh, and *presto!*—seriousness is transformed into fun. As I wrote in *The 10 Smartest Decisions a Woman Can Make Before 40:*

> Play removes us from our normal stressful environment. When you play, you are in a creative, spontaneous, mode; focused on enjoying yourself and other people. In play, you are not focused on your problems or obligations, but on what you are doing in the moment. Having fun in your relationships and friendships keeps them strong. When we have fun together, we create good feelings that later become good memories.

The ability to create fun wherever you are is a skill you can learn. Like all other emotional/psychological skills, it begins within.

SIMPLE PLEASURES

Having fun starts with having the right attitude. The same activity that is hard work one day can be a pleasure the next, because you've figured out how to see it differently. Without humor, life doesn't feel worth living. A sense of humor can help you through the rough times of life, and laughter can change an argument into a reasonable exchange or recharge and refresh you when you're tired. If you know how to create fun for yourself and how to notice when you do it, you can have fun in very simple ways.

Fun is the result of being present in the moment even when (or particularly when!) you're engaged in an ordinary activity, such as strolling in your neighborhood. When you are able to put your full attention on whatever you are doing right now, you are available to have fun when the opportunity arises. It is a very creative process, and it begins within you.

The following exercise will give you a place you can enjoy being with yourself. In that place you can generate the kind of inner peace and intimacy that enhances and develops your creativity.

Build a Retreat

In this exercise you'll practice using your imagination to build a personal retreat. With practice, your retreat will become a place you can go to for centering and refocusing your attention and attitude. You will also develop your creative thinking. In doing this exercise, take care to imagine and develop your sensory impressions in the most vivid detail possible. You will be asked to notice how everything looks, feels, smells, sounds, and tastes. The more completely you can experience all of these sensory details, the more effective you will be at being present. It is important to take the time to get your senses involved in the process. With practice, your sensory awareness will deepen until the sights, sounds, feelings, smells, and tastes of the world around you are quite sharp and have a strong impact.

Read the following instructions into a tape recorder or take turns with a friend and read them aloud for each other. Your imagination will then be free to roam and to picture scenes in ever-increasing detail without having to stop and interrupt yourself to read each new instruction.

1. CHOOSE A SCENE. Imagine a favorite place, relaxing and private, where you can enjoy being alone. It might be a tropical beach, a favorite room, a forest waterfall, a porch swing, a luxurious hotel suite, or a favorite spot in your home. As you think of the scene, notice whether it feels "real" to you, because you'll contrast this perception to how you feel afterward. You will probably feel distant from it and somewhat detached at this point, before you use your senses.

2. DEVELOP YOUR VISUAL IMAGE. Get comfortably seated, relax your body, close your eyes, and use your imagination to see the scene you have chosen in as much detail as possible, but don't strain or struggle to see it. Allow the scene to unfold and add

details as you think of them. It's not important to create a perfect, lifelike image, just imagine the scene. Think about what it looks like. Is it outdoors or indoors? Is it day or night? What colors do you see? Are there flowers, trees, rocks, furniture, or decorations? As you invoke the remaining senses with the subsequent steps of the exercise, the scene will become clearer.

3. PICTURE YOURSELF IN THE SCENE. Now imagine yourself in your scene and look around you: are you standing, sitting, or lying down? What objects in the scene are near you? Which ones are at a distance? What are you wearing? How do you look?

4. USE YOUR SENSE OF TOUCH. Imagine how it feels: are you lying on grass, sitting in a favorite chair, standing on a city street, or perhaps dangling your bare feet in a running brook? What does the air feel like? Is it clear and rich, the way it is after a rain, or is it the close, heavy air of summer? Is a breeze moving against your skin, blowing your hair? Are you warm or cool? Are your clothes rough or smooth, tight or loose? Or are you wearing clothes at all?

5. USE YOUR SENSE OF HEARING. Imagine the sounds: is there traffic noise, a radio, music, voices in another room, floors creaking, a fan whirring, birds chirping, water running, or the wind blowing?

6. USE YOUR SENSE OF SMELL. What aromas do you smell? Can you smell food cooking, flowers, animals, rain on the breeze, cleaning products, pipe tobacco?

7. USE YOUR SENSE OF TASTE. Do you taste anything? The mouth-watering taste of delicious food or coffee, the dusty taste of an old attic, or the sweet, metallic flavor of rain?

8. REINVOKE ALL YOUR SENSES. Absorb the sensory feelings of your retreat—sights, sounds, touch, smells, and tastes—and relax fully into the scene so you can experience your retreat in as much sensory detail as possible before going on to the next step.

9. PERFECT YOUR RETREAT. Look around your special place and see how it suits you. Improve and change it to please yourself. This is your personal haven, so make it as comfortable and pleasant as possible. Would you prefer more privacy? More light? More green grass and trees? A cozier place to sit? Try out various combinations; you can change them back if you don't like them. When you feel it is just the way you want it, go on to the next step.

10. NOTICE HOW YOU FEEL. How do you feel? Do you feel more relaxed, calmer, and more secure? Have your thoughts slowed and become quieter? Do you feel emotions you have not felt for a while, such as nostalgia, peace, sadness, happiness, love for others or for yourself? You may even notice that as you developed the sensory images of your retreat, the sounds and sensations of your real world have receded. You may even feel more "present" in your mental retreat than in your actual surroundings. Relax a few moments and let these feelings sink in to get the full benefit of the calm, relaxing peace of your retreat. Then slowly transfer your attention back to your physical surroundings, and then, slowly and gently, open your eyes.

You can use a visualization like this at any time to turn a stressful or boring moment into a pleasure.

When **Sally** feels overwhelmed with the pressure and responsibility of owning her own business, she visualizes one of her favorite travel destinations. Picturing herself at the Taj Mahal, on a beach in Tahiti, or sipping café au lait on the Boulevard St. Germain in Paris is like taking a mini-vacation. After a few minutes of intense visualization, she is refreshed and ready to resume work. When she actually travels, she finds she pays more attention to the sensory clues of her surroundings, noticing colors, sights, smells, and the feel of the air. By focusing her awareness on the details of her environment, her experiences have become more pleasurable and more memorable.

Practicing visualizations like this will help you learn to "tune in" wherever you are, notice your surroundings with your senses, and stay present in the moment. In addition, you have created a mental and emotional haven where you can retreat any time you need a break from life's stresses and strains. Although this visualization in itself may not fit your definition of "fun," it will help you relax and let go of stress, so that being spontaneous and having fun will feel more natural.

As you get more familiar with your internal sense of safety and peace, your idea of what is fun will change. "If you want to be happy for six months, get married," says a Chinese proverb; "if you want to be happy for the rest of your life, learn to garden."

With all the responsibility of caring for her parents, **Julie** has little time for leisure, but she found that planting a few petunias in pots on the back porch helped cheer her up and relax her.

Tending to her potted flowers for a moment each day helps remind her of the beauty in the world and the blessings we tend to take for granted. She calls it her "tuning-in moment."

When you have an understanding of what it is to be present, to fully experience whatever you are doing, the most mundane tasks and pastimes take on new meaning. If you practice experiencing your everyday life with the full participation of all your senses, as in the previous exercise, you'll find that each moment becomes richer, more alive, and more exciting than ever before. What could feel better than that? And if it feels that good, isn't it fun? Consider the new possibilities of really being wherever you are at that very moment.

"When you're in flow, you may be stretching yourself tremendously, but at the end you feel like you have relaxed physically," writes Mihaly Csikszentmihalyi in *Flow: The Psychology of Optimal Experience.* Csikszentmihalyi also states:

Flow requires investing all your attention in what you are doing. That acts as a kind of barrier against all the preoccupations that we have in life. If the relaxation has an activity look to it . . . that could be flow. . . . It means paying attention to what is happening around you so that you notice things, care about what happens, and forget yourself in the process. Whatever you are doing becomes very absorbing and interesting. When you get up in the morning, you try to figure out what about this day is going to be interesting or meaningful. You try to enjoy your breakfast, brushing your teeth, or whatever, you find a way to have an interesting conversation. That is what makes life worth living, not the things you will achieve tomorrow or the day after.

THE POWER OF A GOOD LAUGH

We all enjoy a good laugh, but you might not realize how powerful the gift of laughter can be. If you are the person who makes your children and friends laugh, if you can pull a spouse or sibling out of the doldrums with a funny quip, or if you can see the humor in even difficult situations, then you are able to bring the great gift of humor to the people around you. "A touch of folly," advised the famous French philosopher François La Rochefoucauld, "is needed if we are to extricate ourselves successfully from some of the hazards of life."

Laurie's friend Sylvia phoned and said, "I miss you, I haven't spoken to you in several days." "Thanks for the compliment," Laurie said. "I have been really busy, but I've missed you, too." They talked for a few minutes, and Sylvia said, "I don't know why, but I have the blues today, I'm feeling a little down." Laurie replied mischievously, "That's because you've missed me." Sylvia laughed. "You're right! I feel better already."

The simple act of laughing with a friend can turn the whole day around for both of you. Laughter in the midst of problems brings hope that things will get better. It is widely believed that laughter even boosts the immune system and helps heal disease.

You probably remember the story of *Saturday Review* editor Norman Cousins, who insisted in his memoir, *The Anatomy of an*

Illness, that he healed himself of a life-threatening illness through laughter. Subsequent research has confirmed that laughter and friendships enhance health, well-being, and longevity. Educator Sabina White of the Santa Barbara Laughter Project writes:

> There's no question, that laughter has both physiological and psychological benefits. Like exercise, it reduces tension . . . laughter gives the body a sort of mini-workout. Like exercising, laughing involves virtually every major system of the body. Laughter is a cathartic. . . . We all feel better when we laugh. . . . Why not laugh more and feel better?

"Yes, it's actually a serious fact that laughter is good medicine," reports RealAge.com:

> Numerous studies have shown that a good guffaw delivers many health benefits, such as lowering blood pressure and releasing endorphins—chemicals in the brain that can ease pain and make you feel good. Laughter also is thought to improve circulation, stimulate the nervous system, strengthen the heart, and enhance the immune system.

Knowing how to find the funny side of a situation, or how to make a silly face at the perfect moment, can be the greatest gift you bestow. America's most beloved and lasting humorists—such as Will Rogers, Woody Allen, Bill Cosby, Whoopi Goldberg, and Lily Tomlin—all have an ability to see and express our common experiences, the silliness we all share, in a gentle, non-aggressive manner. You may not be able to match their quick wit, but you can bring into your life the fresh breeze of laughter. Through humor we can make every day more pleasant and grease the wheels of interaction with friends, family, and business associates. Knowing what is funny to yourself and the people close to you—what comedians you like, what movies, books, or humor writers amuse you—becomes a great tool for revitalizing and adding delight to all your connections with people.

THE JOY OF BALANCE

The key to having fun *and* getting work done is learning to balance both experiences. The following guidelines will help you to balance work and play in your life.

Guidelines for Having Fun

1. PLAY EVERY DAY. Make enough space in your schedule for activities that relax you and give you pleasure.

2. KNOW WHAT'S FUN FOR YOU. Looking back at your life, pick out the most fun times. Focus on what pleased you most rather than the most elaborate events. What were you doing? Who were you with? Have you ever had fun alone? What makes you smile? What relaxes and refreshes you? Make a "fun list" so when you want to relax and have a good time, you'll have some ideas at your fingertips.

3. FIND PARTNERS FOR FUN. Identify your most likely partners for fun. Your partners might be your three-year-old grandchild or

your friend of twenty years. They might be the women at your aerobics class or neighbors. Make a list of the people you know who take the time to play and enjoy life. Make sure you often spend time with these people.

4. LAUGH A LOT. Think about what makes you laugh and do as much of it as possible. When you have an evening at home alone, rent your favorite funny movie. The research quoted earlier in this book shows that laughter is not only fun, it can improve your health!

5. SHOOT FROM THE HIP. As contradictory as it may seem, practice spontaneity. Do more things without planning in advance. Allow yourself to crack a joke, make a funny comment, or be silly some of the time.

6. PLAN FOR FUN. You don't *have* to clean the house every Saturday, instead, make sure you regularly do what you know you'll enjoy. Invite your "fun people" over, play a game that makes you laugh, or cheer for your favorite team to get your energy going.

7. HAVE A SILLY CELEBRATION. Celebrate your (or a friend's) un-birthday any day you want. Throw a middle-of-the-week party. Invite a friend out to lunch, but make it a surprise with a picnic in the park. Fill your house with balloons for no reason at all. Send funny cards to people you know because it's Wednesday. Pop the cork on a virtual bottle of champagne with your online friends. Call a friend up and sing a silly song over the phone.

Devise more ways to have fun on your own and use them all frequently. At this stage of your life, you deserve to have the richest experiences possible; to have the joy and healing experiences of fun, friendship, laughter, and sensory experience; to enjoy your life to the fullest. As you have seen here, a change in your attitude can change how much fun you have. You can energize and motivate yourself by allowing yourself to celebrate small goals. By deciding now to have more fun, and to utilize every type of fun, you'll maximize your joy in life.

CHAPTER 9

Why Are You Here?: Decide to Create Meaning in Your Life

> *It isn't until you come to a spiritual understanding of who you are—*
> *not necessarily a religious feeling, but deep down, the spirit within—*
> *that you can begin to take control.*
>
> —Oprah Winfrey

As a therapist I watch many of my clients pass through somewhat similar stages of personal growth. First, they explore and understand the origins of the stresses in their life. Next, they work on learning to manage those stresses (both internal and external) successfully. They will often then reach a stage of, "What now?"— which prompts a desire to search for meaning. As you mature, what you can accomplish in life begins to be less important than what your life *means.* Sooner or later all of us question the meaning of life, and the sooner we get to it, the better chance we have of finding a satisfactory answer. Each of us is different, and each of us has a different idea of what "satisfaction" and "meaning" are—but we know when we feel them.

Now that you've reached forty, you're probably feeling that creating meaning and joy in your life is a now-or-never proposition.

That belief is actually the definition of the infamous "midlife crisis" many people experience between the ages of forty and fifty. Many women deny themselves satisfaction by not giving themselves credit for their accomplishments. If you have a tendency to say, "I was only a housewife" or "I just did a meaningless job" or "I never got far in school," you're probably undervaluing what you've contributed to the world. Whether you acknowledge your past achievements or not, though, you may wake up one day asking, "What does it all mean? Why am I doing all this? What's the point?"

You needn't be dismayed if you are feeling this way, because asking those questions is the beginning of creating the meaningful life you crave. As a woman of the baby-boomer generation, you have experienced a lot of change in your lifetime. You are part of the generation of women who dared to dream they could be whatever they wanted. If you have any unfinished business, unrealized dreams, or regrets, this is your chance to make sure your life is everything you always wanted it to be.

Marian says, "I spent my earlier years being so busy working and raising Mandy that I never thought much about spirituality beyond going to church on Sunday. Now that my life is less chaotic, Mandy is older, and I'm more financially secure, I am beginning to think about the meaning of my life. I got great satisfaction from my role as a mother, but I've begun to be troubled by the plight of low-income single mothers and their children. I've decided to see what I can do with my legal training and education to help them."

Perhaps your parents dreamed of retirement and sliding gently into a peaceful old age surrounded by grandchildren—but that would not be enough for you. It's time, if you haven't done so already, to figure out what a life of satisfaction and joy—a life you can truly feel grateful to be living—would be.

WHAT IS YOUR LIFE ALL ABOUT?

A search for meaning is just that—a search. It's a discovery process, a learning experience, and a creative event. Although some women undergo dramatic events, such as a near-death experience, that seem to make everything fall into place, most of us don't find meaning in that way. Instead, understanding begins early in life and grows gradually, as you attempt to make sense of all the joys and pains of living. At some point you may feel a need to go on an active quest for meaning. This is what Dr. Bernie Siegel calls "finding your job on earth" in his book, *Peace, Love and Healing:*

> Whatever your age, if you learn to listen, your inner voice will speak to you about your path . . . your "job on earth." This wisdom that is directing you from within is your birthright . . . an inner message, an inner awareness, that says, "This is your path, this is how you can be the best human being possible." If you follow it, you will achieve your full growth and full potential as a human being. . . .

The costs of denying your heart's desire are far greater than the costs of following it. "To find in ourselves what makes life worth living is risky business," writes researcher Marsha Sinetar in *Ordinary People as Monks and Mystics,* "for it means that once we know it we must seek it. It also means that without it life will be valueless." Taking the risk, letting yourself follow your heart and your imagination, leads to discovery. Discovering the meaning of your life will lead you to places you've only dreamed of.

This exercise will help you examine who you are from a different vantage point—as an all-knowing Being might see you—to give you a broader, more detached, and wiser (not to mention kinder and gentler) view of yourself and your life. The goal is to alter your perceptions of yourself and your talents, qualities, and circumstances.

Finding Personal Meaning and Purpose

What if life is organized to some grand plan and an infinitely wise and creative Being designed your own unique mix of traits to accomplish a specific goal? What would be your purpose in the plan? If you were designed for a special purpose, you would be given inherent talents and qualities to help you do the job. Review the kind of person you are and the abilities that come naturally to you (even if they sometimes get you into trouble). What would people who know you say about your outstanding qualities? Let your imagination go wherever it wants to when you answer these questions in your journal. Use the following questions to inspire and challenge you to choose your own talents, qualities, desires, and circumstances.

- What are your personal qualities?
  - Are you friendly, open, or outgoing?
  - Are you solitary, quiet, or reserved?
  - Are you communicative?
  - Are you a good listener and receptive?
  - Are you a dreamer or an intellectual?

Are you a conscientious, productive worker?

Are you physically active, the outdoorsy type?

Are you relaxed or meditative?

Are you practical, thrifty, or cautious?

Are you courageous, bold, or experimental?

Are you fun or enthusiastic?

Are you imaginative or creative?

Are you funny or witty?

Are you original or innovative (sometimes called "weird")?

Do you work or play better alone or with others?

Do you enjoy structure or openness more?

Do you enjoy productivity or play more?

Add to the list in your journal any personality traits you have that I did not include.

- What are your talents?

  Are you musically inclined? Can you play an instrument or sing? Do you compose, appreciate, or critique music?

  Are you a skilled communicator? Are you a good conversationalist or writer? Are you a good public speaker or teacher?

  Are you artistic? Can you paint or draw? Can you sculpt or throw pottery? Do you dance, act, or direct?

  Do you have intellectual talents? Are you good at math, spatial relations, computer games, or programming? Do you have a knack for solving puzzles?

  Are you good with your hands? Do you excel at a craft, needlework, or carpentry? Do you have mechanical gifts?

Do you enjoy athletic activity? Do you like to play individual or team sports? Do you coach or referee? Are you a big fan?

Are you a skilled negotiator? Are you good at helping people understand each other? Do you enjoy brainstorming solutions to problems?

Are you a nurturer? Do you excel at caring for children, the sick, the elderly, or friends?

Do you have an ability to get things done? Are you efficient, dedicated, determined? Do you follow through on projects?

Add to your list any other talents that you have.

- What are your desires?

    Would you like to clean up the environment?

    Is there a political cause that interests you?

    Would you like to express yourself musically or artistically?

    Do you want to travel?

    Would you like to make a quilt?

    Do you dream of doing Shakespeare in the park or of making a film?

    Would you like to be successful financially?

    Do you want to become a healer or health-care worker?

    Do you want to care for a child or children?

    Would you like to grow a garden?

    Do you want to follow a spiritual path?

    Would you like to love and be loved?

    Do you want to fly an airplane?

Do you want to help animals or save human lives?

Do you want to get a college degree?

Do you want to write a book or teach?

Include any of your desires (no matter how fanciful) that don't appear on this list.

- What circumstances seem to repeat in your life?

    Do people tell you their life stories (whether or not you ask)?

    Do you often wind up teaching, talking to, organizing, or leading groups?

    Are you drawn to churches, museums, forests, bookstores, farms, schools, hospitals, theaters, or factories?

    Do you find yourself repeatedly working with computers, plants, paintbrushes, horses, babies, heavy machinery, or microscopes?

    Do you have to find new jobs because your career self-destructs?

    Do you find yourself thinking about: helping AIDS babies or the League of Women Voters, writing a play or novel, going to Brazil, having sex, protecting human rights, or living in the woods?

    Do you often have the feeling that there's something you're "supposed" to be doing, but you don't know what it is?

    Write down any other recurring thoughts or circumstances.

- Rewrite the following sentence, filling in the blanks with the talents, qualities, desires, and circumstances you wrote in your journal. You may have several words for each blank in the sentence. You may want to write out the sentence several times, with several variations. Experiment with it, until it feels right.

> I _____ *(your name)* was designed to be a *(quality)* person who can _____ *(talent)* and I find myself _____ *(circumstance)* often, because I am supposed to _____ *(desire)*.

This exercise, if you do it conscientiously, will begin to create change in your life. If you allow yourself to fantasize about your life purpose, your acceptance of personal characteristics that you may have ignored or undervalued in your past will grow, and you'll create a new open-mindedness about the meaning of events in your life, which will increase your satisfaction.

Guidelines for Evaluating Your Purpose

How do you know your purpose is the true meaning of your life? Once you have an idea of what your life purpose might be, you can test it using three criteria: results, experience, and ethics. The following guidelines will help you evaluate the effectiveness and suitability of your life purpose.

1. RESULTS. By paying attention to the results, the way a scientist conducting a lab experiment would, you can know if you're on the "right track" in your life. To evaluate your results, consider your stress level, your finances, your relationships, the time you spend at leisure and work, and whether the steps you

need to follow to achieve your life purpose are going smoothly or with difficulty.

Even with the best of intentions, sometimes your experiment with meaningful living will go wrong or your results may be mixed and inconclusive. When you get a negative result, you might want to ask yourself the following questions:

- Is this an important result? One negative result, amid a lot of positive results, may not be important. A certain number of negative results are to be expected. Every successful woman has stories of failure and rejection. Like them, you can just reevaluate, correct errors, and try again. In this way, you can learn from negative results and persevere.

- How does this result reflect my original idea? Is the result so different from what I expected that I want to reevaluate what I am doing in life, or could it just give me some new ideas about how to do it more effectively? Your negative results, like those of a scientist in his lab, can just help point you in a more effective direction.

In addition to the concrete, observable results, there are other, internal results that can help you decide whether your purpose is right for you. Your disappointment, dissatisfaction, anger, grief, frustration, and fear are all clues about whether or not your life is satisfying and healthy for you. This is equally true of your positive emotions—happiness, fulfillment, contentment, and excitement.

2. EXPERIENCE. The second criterion for evaluating your life purpose is your experience. As you experience bringing your idea

of your purpose toward fulfillment, both the original idea and the final expression of it will change. In the beginning, your purpose is a dream, a fantasy, and you can only imagine it. Any dream is bound to need some adjustment as you begin to make it a reality.

Laurie's dream of using her medical education to care for the terminally ill took a long time to realize. In the beginning, she had dreams of running her own hospice, but as she learned more, she realized that she didn't care for the administrative duties, and her dream changed to working for a hospital that ran a hospice program.

Your main purpose will evolve with your experience, along with every little goal you strive toward. Only if your idea of your original goal is so rigid that you cannot accept the need to adapt it and make it more realistic or more possible for you to accomplish do you need to reevaluate it as your life purpose.

3. ETHICS. No doubt your life purpose entails living by ethical standards. Such standards imposed by or derived from society can never be completely right for you or fully match your personal criteria. It is gratifying to live by your internal values. In his book *Honoring the Self,* psychologist Dr. Nathaniel Branden calls this "living by one's own mind." According to Branden, "[W]e do not attempt to live by unthinking conformity and the suspension of independent critical judgment. We take responsibility for the ideas we accept and the values by which we guide our actions."

Ethics are standards you choose to follow to make your life worth living and to maintain your self-esteem. Being ethical requires evaluating your own life and actions, and it requires independent thought rather than blind obedience. Personal ethics help you define unacceptable behavior and give you the strength to resist it, regardless of whether other people find the same conduct permissible.

Once you become aware of and develop your personal ethics, you become your own guide and teacher. The input of supportive friends can give you another viewpoint from which to evaluate your goals and your purpose; however, the final judgment of the rightness of your actions and the merits of your life purpose belongs to you.

DEVELOP YOUR PERSPECTIVE— LOOK AT YOUR LIFE FROM ANOTHER ANGLE

This exercise is a favorite of many of my female clients and a very effective tool to help you look at your own life and your decisions from a different and valuable perspective. Although it appeared in *The 10 Smartest Decisions a Woman Can Make Before 40,* I feel that it is so useful for women of all ages that I adapted it for inclusion here. The decisions you make today affect the rest of your life, and you are ultimately the only person to whom you are accountable and for whom you are responsible. Every new decision is truly a new life's resolution.

The Wise Woman

In this guided fantasy, designed to help you achieve a helpful perspective on your own future, you create an adviser for your life decisions. Ask a friend to read the following to you or record it on audiotape. The exercise should be read very slowly and quietly.

Relax, breathe slowly and comfortably, get comfortable in your chair, and picture a woman of seventy or more. This woman is just the kind of older woman you admire, the one you would like to become. She is financially secure, in good health, surrounded by people who care about her, good friends and family. . . . She has lots of interests to keep her busy, and she stays quite active. . . . Introduce yourself to this woman . . . as she gives you her name, you notice it's the same as yours—she is you, later in life. . . . Make an agreement with this ideal older self that you will get advice from her about what decisions you need to make, as life goes on, to live up to her healthy and happy state of being. Continue your conversation with her as long as you wish, and ask her what her secret is for living to such a lovely old age.

Check out your decisions regularly by using your "wise woman." For example, how does this inner counselor react to your life purpose? At her age, will you look back on it and think it was worth it? Does your wise woman approve? Does she think your choice will last? What is the difference between what you regard as important and what she regards as important?

FINDING MEANING IN LOSS

All the experiences of your life, especially the difficult ones, have taught you valuable skills. Learning to use what you've learned to help others can create meaning out of pain.

The duality of life is seen in many belief systems. For example, Buddhist philosophers note that poisonous plants and venoms become healing medicines with careful processing. Every trial you face has something to teach you and can become a source of wisdom. Your inner wise woman knows this well.

By this time in your life you may have experienced a lot of loss. You may have lost elderly relatives, such as grandparents or parents, a beloved friend, a partner, or a sibling. You may have experienced the profound grief of losing a child. The grieving process is an amazing education. You learn that you can survive even the most devastating loss as you experience what psychiatrist Elisabeth Kübler-Ross termed the "stages of grief"—denial, anger, bargaining, depression, and acceptance.

Although the loss of her mother was quite painful, **Laurie** has found a powerful use for her experience in helping her dying hospice patients and their families. Because of the depth of her own experience, she can empathize with, understand, and offer support for others' grief.

Like Laurie, you know from your experience that the stages of grief come and go—not in a neat, linear way, but all jumbled up. You learn that grief is initially intense, but if you express it and allow yourself to honor the grieving process, it begins to subside over time. You learn that certain words and gestures by friends and relatives help heal, and other responses increase your pain. You learn the difference between self-pity and grieving. You know what it feels like to be blindsided by an excruciating stab of pain because you unexpectedly come across a reminder of the person you lost: a scent, a phrase, an object, a picture, an old movie that brings up memories. Knowing how to grieve effectively is an essential life skill—we are all going to lose more and more people as we age. Having skill at grieving is valuable to you because it helps you manage the difficult times and to find meaning in loss.

Out of your experience you can, moreover, become a guide through this life passage for your family and friends. You may even want to use what you know to help strangers in need, through hospice work or grief groups.

Both your joyful and painful life experiences have important lessons for you, which you can incorporate into your value system and use to enrich your life.

FINDING MEANING IN YOUR VALUES

As you live longer and gain more experience, you learn that certain things give more meaning to your existence. If your religious beliefs or philosophy of living are comforting to you, they eventually will become the basis for most of your decisions. Research shows that people who are connected through others by the same belief system are happier, healthier, and report more satisfaction with their lives than those who are not. "We are creatures of community," writes Dr. Dean Ornish in *Love and Survival: The Scientific Basis for the Healing Power of Intimacy.* Ornish states:

> Those individuals, societies, and cultures who learned to take care of each other, to love each other, and to nurture relationships with each other during the past several hundred thousand years were more likely to survive than those

who did not. . . . In short, anything that promotes a sense of isolation often leads to illness and suffering. Anything that promotes a sense of love and intimacy, connection and community is healing.

Living according to your values is not always easy, because modern society often encourages you to put status, appearance, and the accumulation of money and consumer goods above ethics and values. The influence of a caring community, such as family, friends, a religious group, or even the members of a recovery program, can be a tremendous force in an individual's life. They can help you fight off the shallow values of the consumer culture and remain true to the values within.

Philosophical or Religious Values

If you find that you have strayed from the things that are most important to you, there is no better time in your life to reembrace your values. Following a religion, a philosophy of life, or a spiritual framework can impart meaning to all your actions. In fact, having a clear set of values often helps you make many decisions.

Involvement in a self-help program for children of alcoholics really helped **Rose** define her personal values. Growing up in an atmosphere where the adults were often out of control was very confusing to Rose as a child, and she needed someone to help her understand what "normal" adult behavior was. In the beginning she followed faithfully the practices taught by her group, but as she became more comfortable, she began to develop her own behavioral guidelines. As she learned from experience and gained wisdom, these personal guidelines grew into a core system of values. She no longer needed to rigidly follow the teachings of her program, for she now understood what makes life meaningful and rewarding for herself. Rose has found a value system that works in her life, and her desire to become a counselor and learn to be effective at helping people grows from that foundation. She is no longer tempted when a member of her family "invites" her to get drunk, or fight or gossip with them, because she knows this conduct doesn't get the results she wants in her life.

Like Rose, you can build your life around a life-changing dynamic, or you may choose a traditional religion. Many adults rediscover their faith in the religion of their upbringing. Others discover that a different belief system is more fulfilling to them. Participation in an organized religion is the framework for many people's expression of their spirituality. You may want to revisit the church in which you were raised or explore an alternative religion. On the other hand, if your thinking is different from the more common belief systems, you might choose a meditative discipline such as transcendental meditation or Sufism or a philosophy such as wicca or Taoism.

The rituals of religion can help you clarify and strengthen your inner values. Incorporating prayer or meditation into your everyday life creates a constant reminder of the values you want to maintain. Some women prefer to reinforce their spirituality through regular reading or similar exercise such as studying the Torah or the Christian philosophers, using a divination guide such as the Tarot or I Ching, or taking classes provided by spiritual advisers. Applying the principles of your chosen ideology to your everyday tasks and doing your best to live up to its precepts naturally imparts meaning to all you do.

Laurie finds tremendous meaning and richness in using her medical skills in hospice work. Helping her patients choose their own course of treatment, teaching them about the options for pain relief, and sharing the experience of their terminal illnesses with them is deeply rewarding for her. Although many people think her work is grim, Laurie finds great joy in knowing she's helping people who are truly in need, in a world that usually spurns them. "I'm not religious in the ordinary sense—I work most Sundays and don't go to church," explains Laurie, "but every day I am overwhelmed with gratitude for my ability, which I believe comes from God, and the opportunity to be of service to those who need me so much."

Artistic Values

Perhaps for you, meaning and value lie in the arts as an adjunct to, or in lieu of, a religious practice. Dance, painting, pottery, music, and other artistic pursuits can also be forms of meditation. Creating beauty, evoking emotion, and expressing social problems through artistic avenues can be invaluable ways to contribute to life and society. Such artistic expression might be connected to religious or spiritual values. Regardless, if it has potent meaning for you, it will infuse your life with energy and purpose. Teaching the arts to others can also be very therapeutic and healing.

Karen loves singing jazz, but she also gets great satisfaction and meaning from singing with her church choir at convalescent hospitals and charity functions, and she takes a lot of pleasure in teaching music to the children in Sunday school.

As you infuse whatever you're doing—from the smallest task to the largest social cause—with your own artistic expression, you're engaged in what Thomas Moore called "care of the soul":

> If we are going to care for the soul, and if we know that the soul is nurtured by beauty, then we will have to understand beauty more deeply and give it a more prominent place in life. . . . An appreciation of beauty is simply an openness to the power of things to stir the soul. If we can be affected by beauty, then soul is alive and well in us, because the soul's great talent is for being affected. . . . We don't often think of the capacity to be affected as strength, and as the work of a powerful muscle, and yet for the soul . . . this is its toughest work and its main role in our lives.

We all know the feeling Moore describes, when the beauty of a sunset, a majestic natural vista, or a work of art transfixes our attention and causes us to catch our breath. When we respond to beauty or attempt to create it, we feel a connection with the deepest meaning of life.

Social Values

What excites and energizes you may not be religious or artistic at all, but involves social or political values. To work for the environment, human rights, or the betterment of your community or your neighbors can add tremendous meaning to your life. As a volunteer, you can feed soup and sandwiches to the homeless, rock the babies in your local hospital's neonatal ward, speak to schoolchildren about ecology or the arts, visit the elderly or shut-ins, or just be supportive to your friends and family. Or you can find a like-minded group that shares your political or cultural concerns, such as a local, state, or national political campaign, an environmental organization, or a local charity. Perhaps an educational group (such as the League of Women Voters or Mothers Against Drunk Driving, known as MADD), or an art, theater, or history foundation could use your skills as a volunteer. If a social cause means a lot to you, there will be other people who are equally interested. Engaging in this type of activism is also a great way to make new friends—you obviously have something in common with your fellow activists.

With some members of her self-help group, **Rose** began speaking at schools and civic associations about the problems faced by families of alcoholics. She and the others organized the talks because they felt people in their community needed more information about the problem, what to do about it, and the resources that were available to help families cope. Rose got a lot of satisfaction from helping people with her hard-won wisdom and also gained speaking skills that would serve her well in her counseling practice. Because of their shared experience, strong friendships were developed within the group that organized and gave the talks.

For many women, expressing their social values is a gratifying way to enhance the meaning in their lives.

A Spiritual Community

When life gets difficult (and everyone's does, from time to time), a philosophy that gives you a way to understand and endure problems can renew your energy and refresh your spirit. These are the times, also, when a community of people who share your beliefs can be counted on for support, comfort, help, and sound advice.

In addition to the richness a network of loving family and friends offers, a community of like-minded people focused on the ideas and values that give your life meaning can add immeasurable satisfaction to your life. I am choosing to call this "a spiritual community," but it may have little to do with religion. Each of the groups and causes mentioned earlier in this chapter can serve as a community of meaning for you.

If an organized religion has a lot of meaning for you, being involved in a church, synagogue, temple, or other spiritual group with similar aims and beliefs can supply the connections you need and support you in living its values.

A community of people who share values and concerns as well as a spiritual context will help you be more effective, celebrate your accomplishments, and support you in your difficulties. Working together to accomplish something you all value adds extra meaning to your connection, and the shared beliefs become a source of strength in difficult times. Shared accomplishments based on meaning and faith provide lasting satisfaction, as opposed to the temporary thrill of earning more money or buying the latest fad item.

Artistic, social, and spiritual values can be expressed individually or collectively. You may choose to express your spiritual values in your art or by working for a social cause. Regardless of the path you take, deciding to live according to a greater purpose adds meaning and satisfaction to the most everyday tasks and ordinary acts.

CHAPTER 10

Share Your Bounty: Decide to Give Something Back

> *Life begets life. Energy creates energy. It is by spending oneself that one becomes rich.*
>
> —Sarah Bernhardt

Satisfaction and success come not only from what you do, but also from what you contribute. As you look back on your life, you are likely to feel best about the good things you did for others and the positive contributions you have made to your friends, family, children, students, or co-workers, your work itself, and society as a whole.

Some of the most famous and powerful people have realized the value of giving of themselves. "I recognize that the forum I have been given is not to acquire attention and possessions for myself," writes Oprah Winfrey on the Web site www.zukav.com. Winfrey states:

What is the purpose of this attention if it cannot be used for a higher good? I have a contract with the Universe that I'm going to use this attention in the highest way. I am not going to just have fun with it. For me that won't work. There is a much deeper level to it. . . . I think about the wealth that I have acquired and the responsibility I now have to share it in the world in a way that brings honor to people, a greater sense of self-value. I really labor over how best to do this.

As a woman, your traditional societal role is to act as nurturer. Although many of us love to give affection and to care for others, we often feel doing so is our "job." The joy of helping others seems to get lost. When you give yourself freely, deliberately, with "no strings attached," however, you'll find that you enjoy it much more.

As part of her search for meaning, **Karen** got more involved in her church. One Sunday a month, parishioners have taken responsibility for feeding the homeless at a soup kitchen. Karen was reluctant at first to take part, but now she goes faithfully on the designated Sunday and doles out soup and sandwiches she makes herself. "It was uncomfortable at first, too close to the poverty I grew up in, but now I find great satisfaction in helping these people," she says. "Even if I'm only providing one meal a month, it feels like an important contribution to them and to me."

PUTTING YOUR TALENTS TO USE

Creating a more satisfying life begins with valuing your expertise and the wisdom of your years of life experience. You have gained valuable skills and knowledge that you did not have in your early twenties. You may think of your abilities as being work-related, but there are many personal and very useful, skills learned only through experience.

As you undoubtedly have realized from reading this book, I'm a big advocate of recognizing (and using!) the skills that you've gained over the course of your life. Your emotional, intellectual, social, and organizational skills are just as valuable as being good at business, sports, or programming computers. The ability to bring humor to the lives of those around you is a wonderful talent. As I mentioned in the prior chapter, the ability to comfort yourself and others in times of grief is an essential, and extremely useful, skill.

In the exercises you have already recorded in your journal, there are a lot of clues about the skills and talents you have gained throughout your life. Review your journal to discover the gifts you have to give and those that you are giving at present. In the last chapter, you explored creating meaning in your life. In this chapter, you'll add to that meaning by giving back from the resources you have accumulated, both personal and material.

GIVING AND RECEIVING: THE ESSENCE OF THE GROUP DYNAMIC

The most obvious benefit of giving is that when you give, people have a tendency to want to reciprocate. If you have had a pattern of giving too much and not receiving in return, you can create a new pattern—"rebalance"—by learning to receive as effectively as you give. In fact, learning to balance your giving and receiving will help heal old connections with family and friends, and it will help establish new, healthier ones.

By this time in your life, you understand the importance of being connected to others. We have all heard that "it's not what you know, it's who you know." To a large extent it's true: a widespread network can assist you in many ways. A solid network can give you a group of friends that's big enough to meet all your social needs; serve as a resource for business, educational, and personal connections; provide companionship and replacements for lost friends and family; and surround you with peers who will understand your life experiences and support you when you need it.

Working together with others can offer enormous benefits that make life easier and more pleasant. The most effective networks are those in which everyone gives as well as receives. In fact, that is the proper function of any family or group. Groups that don't relate in this way are termed *dysfunctional.* Functional groups support every member and are part of greater networks that connect every member to other groups. When you belong to such groups, your giving comes back to you in ways you can never anticipate or imagine. The following opportunities are presented to stir your imagination and to inspire you to find ways to give back and to receive in new and creative ways.

OPPORTUNITIES FOR GIVING BACK

Giving back doesn't necessarily mean returning favors. Even if you want to give something back to those people who helped you, they may no longer be available or need what you have to give. Finding ways to pass on the help you yourself received can be the most satisfying way to contribute. To maximize your effectiveness, and also your satisfaction, it helps to do research to find where your gifts are most needed and most welcomed. There are opportunities all around you and some farther afield.

GIVING CLOSE TO HOME

Giving back can be very simple, and opportunities can be right around the corner. Look around for ways to be of service that are close to home.

Helping in Your Family

Charity begins at home, so your most appropriate opportunity to help may be within your own family. If you have devoted your time to school or your career earlier in life, there's a good chance you had some support along the way. Perhaps your parents provided financial support and mentoring, your own children and spouse encouraged you and took care of themselves to free up your time, or your siblings gave you emotional support or provided child care. If this is the case, the way to give back may seem obvious. Consider helping your own children or nieces and nephews with tutoring in school and with financial aid for college. Perhaps you can spend more time caring for your aging parents or simply giving emotional support to stressed siblings. In times of sickness or financial crisis, your help can make all the difference.

Sharing good times, special family occasions, and old and new traditions can create memories that last a lifetime. If you appreciate your family, let them know. If you are not tightly connected, try giving back by creating some family gatherings. You may be able to strengthen your bond with some family members, and over time others may decide to join you. Sadly, not all families provide a positive response to loving gestures. If your family doesn't get along well, focus on those members who welcome your help and don't get drawn into family problems. If your family is too small, too far away, or too estranged from you, you may need to find other outlets for giving back.

Laurie's family strongly supported her in medical school. When she wanted to make a change to hospice work, some members of her family were critical, but she concentrated on those who backed her. Now she gives back by helping the younger generation with their tuition and by mentoring them in school.

Helping Friends

Perhaps life will present you with an opportunity to give back to friends. Being there in times of need, helping out in times of illness or bereavement, or just being a sympathetic listener when a friend is stressed can be more valuable to them than you imagine. Sometimes matchmaking or simply introducing your friends to one another can help ease a friend's loneliness. Share your rituals, holidays, laughter, and information. Welcome friends who are alone into your family's good times. As a good friend, you can offer comfort in life's difficult times and be a willing participant in celebrating your friends' successes. Everything you give back to your friends will come back to you multiplied.

Julie's group of friends who are caring for parents or other family members has been her salvation time and again. It feels as good to her to help these friends as it does to get help from them.

Helping Neighbors

Even if you're not close enough to consider them friends, giving back to your neighbors will increase your pleasure and the safety of living in your neighborhood. Why not make an effort to get to know the other residents in your apartment or condo complex or the other homeowners on your block? Neighbors who know each other will usually recognize when things are not right and will call emergency services when they witness vandalism, fires, or theft. If your community has a Neighborhood Watch group, you may want to join it or start one yourself. Your local city councilor's office or the police can give you the information you need about Neighborhood Watch organizations. This is a great way to give back to your neighbors.

Karen's neighbors are a close-knit group, assisting each other with child care, throwing block parties, and protecting each other with a Neighborhood Watch group. Her connection with them has made her happier and more secure in her home.

Helping on the Job

Most women today work outside the home, and your workplace can provide a great opportunity for giving back. In fact, a stressful work environment provides a chance to share your gifts in a way that's simple for you and greatly appreciated by your co-workers. Just being pleasant to those with whom you work or staying calm when everyone around you is in a frenzy can make everyone's day better. Teaching a co-worker "the ropes" is a great informal way to mentor.

One of **Ruth's** favorite tasks at work is training new employees in the corporate systems and procedures. She really enjoys teaching.

Helping to Have Fun

If you have a particular sport or leisure activity you enjoy, your favorite way to have fun can be a way of giving back. As a parent or grandparent, you can organize family picnics, holidays, or trips to the zoo or a Disney film. Whether or not you have a family of your own, you can organize a ball game, talent show, or art exhibition for your friends' children or the kids on your block. Or use your love of games and activities to help the elderly or anyone who is lonely or isolated.

Mary's teaching experience has given her a lot of resources for helping groups of children have fun. She decided to give several of her friends and family members a day off, by looking after their children for the afternoon. She took the children to the zoo and had a picnic lunch for all of them. They all had a great time, and Mary enjoyed using her expertise to have fun with her own family.

GIVING FARTHER AFIELD

If you have the energy and ambition to make a bigger statement with your giving, try looking a little farther afield, at opportunities in your community, or in local and national organizations.

Community Opportunities

Every community has wonderful programs that could use your talents and experience. If you look around, you'll find a huge variety of social and professional organizations that will be thrilled to have what you can provide. You can help single mothers, or you can mentor younger women in their careers, get involved in local politics, the arts, your church, or in helping children, the homeless, or the elderly. You can teach whatever skills you have or apply them directly to a project that interests you. Many programs will provide free training in certain skills. As soon as you identify the gifts you have to give, you'll see there are many venues in place with people eager for your abilities.

MOTHER'S HELPER. If you're a mother, perhaps you can envision some product, service, or some knowledge you needed when your children were younger. Out of that awareness you can teach classes or develop products or services that mothers will welcome with open arms. As an alternative, you may decide on a simpler solution—to offer to take another mom's child to the playground with your own (or even if yours are grown), to give a mom an hour off while you read a story to the kids, or to help a neighbor's child who's struggling with math or with reading.

Ruth got a great deal of satisfaction from her involvement in the PTA while her children were in school. She still has contact with many of the younger mothers she advised, and she loves answering their questions about parenting.

HELPING THROUGH POLITICS. Are you aware of the problems in your community? By getting involved in local politics you can prevent your neighborhood from deteriorating, create more parks, care for the environment, help the unfortunate, or keep the community crime rate down. Volunteer at your local city councilor's office, attend city council meetings, or work on a campaign or a local political cause you believe in.

Since **Sally** began working out of her home, she's become more aware of the needs of her community. She's been very active, making her neighbors aware of community issues and keeping in touch with her city council office, where she gets a lot of the information she needs to be effective. She worked with her neighbors to make the alley behind their houses a one-way street, reducing the traffic and the danger of accidents in the narrow passage. Her neighbors have been very cooperative and appreciate Sally's organizational efforts.

SOCIAL, RELIGIOUS, AND SERVICE ORGANIZATIONS. Social, religious, and service organizations abound in every community, including churches, mosques, and synagogues; charitable organizations such as the Red Cross and the Salvation Army; and social-service groups, including Boys and Girls Clubs. If you're already connected with a religious or service organization, getting involved simply means volunteering for tasks that appeal to you. If you don't have a connection already, your community may have a volunteer-services office that can help you decide which is the best place to use your talents, or your local newspaper may publish a list of volunteer opportunities. With a little exploring, you're bound to find a useful and gratifying way to give of yourself.

Karen chooses to give back to the church that helped her so much when she needed it. She uses her musical talent and volunteers at the soup kitchen. Karen's favorite way to contribute to other church members is to be available to counsel young single mothers. She knows the types of challenges they face and has great ideas on budgeting and how to manage a job and a family.

BE A MENTOR. If you have years of expertise in your field, you probably are involved with some of the many professional organizations in your work. Perhaps you are a member of a union, a bar association, a business-networking group such as your chamber of commerce, or a professional society like the American Medical Association or the American Association of Marriage and Family Therapy. Through these job-related organizations, you can teach the hard-won skills you have mastered over the years in your profession. You can offer classes or workshops in your field, mentor younger people one-on-one, or even represent your career at "career days" in local grade schools. In my two professions, as a psychotherapist and as a writer, I have received a lot of help from others, and I do what I can to pass on that support to newcomers in the field. I've developed rewarding relationships with colleagues in the California Association of Marriage and Family Therapists and in the American Society of Journalists and Authors. The exchange of energy seems to happen so quickly that I'm not always sure whether I'm on the giving or the receiving end of the cycle. Either way, the mutual sharing feels great.

If you have benefited from membership in a work-related organization, you can give back by joining a committee or running for office. In this way you can work to realize your ideas of how the organization might be more valuable to its members and the community at large. You can put your expertise to use interpreting legal changes that affect your field or by disseminating information about new jobs, products, developments, or markets; by engaging speakers and developing programs relating to your profession; and by personally helping younger people who are just getting started.

By giving back in this way, you'll get the satisfaction of passing on your expertise and the "street smarts" of your profession and of seeing younger people thrive with your guidance and support (perhaps the help you wished you had had when you were their age). You'll get the chance to realize your ideas of how working in your profession can be more rewarding.

BE A RESOURCE FOR A COLLEGE OR UNIVERSITY. You might want to share your knowledge with special-interest groups at your local college. Computer, art, theater, or foreign-language groups, the school newspaper, honors organizations, and campus political or human-rights organizations need your wisdom and expertise. Whether you can fix their computer equipment, teach social and networking skills or practical business skills, you will find that your know-how is welcome, and you'll enjoy being around the students and teachers.

Marian affiliated herself with her local law school's legal-aid clinic. Each semester she serves as a resource for students handling cases that are going to court. She enjoys her time with the students and gets a chance to assist both them and their clients.

On campus, you can assist faculty members who have similar interests in special programs and events or work side by side with students to help them develop their career potential. You'll also keep abreast of new developments that will add to your effectiveness as a mentor and enjoy passing on your professional or personal experience to those who can benefit from it. The student-affairs office will help you find the proper place to volunteer, or you can call the department you're interested in.

Through family, friends, and community resources, you can give back emotionally by comforting those in need, using your special talents and gifts, and teaching from your expertise. At the same time, you get to make connections with people who have much in common with you, and, ultimately, you'll receive so much more than you are giving. Whether you want to stay close to home or to venture out and change the whole world, getting connected with networks can indeed change your *own* world for the better.

Giving Through National Networks

Service organizations often have national networks, and you can even run for a national office, to give back on a very much larger scale.

Laurie belongs to medical and hospice associations worldwide, and through them she has a wonderful resource for information, personnel, and peer connections. She also gets to share what she learns in working with her patients with other hospice physicians around the world. Because she has served as an officer, she is known by members everywhere and finds the mutual exchange among hospice doctors around the world very useful and gratifying.

A national organization may also have funds available for grants, scholarship programs, or other programs you can design and carry out. The far-reaching influence of these organizations can make it possible for you to help on a scale you never dreamed of.

If you have a burning desire to help remedy a problem, you can begin by connecting with a concerned national organization, such as Habitat for Humanity, the Hunger Project, or Mothers Against Drunk Driving (MADD) or by a funding source such as a foundation or national charity. By volunteering and becoming known to members, you will get support for your own helpful ideas and thoughts.

RECEIVING FROM GIVING BACK

According to RealAge.com, studies show that volunteering actually can help to keep you healthy. People who spend time volunteering report that they feel a high level of satisfaction in life and an improved level of overall health. So, donating your time has a host of benefits—providing you keep your giving in balance with taking care of yourself. The opportunities to give back whatever you've received in your life are endless. You can give on a small scale to the people around you, or you can get connected with organizations and give as widely as you want. To be truly satisfying, whatever you choose to give back should grow out of your personal values, talents, and inspirations.

To give back effectively, you must remain focused on your purpose. Once you decide what you want to give and what effect you hope to create, you set an intention. By keeping that goal in mind you will notice the opportunities and people who can help you achieve what you want to do.

Giving back to your family, your community, and your profession (using the groups and networks available to reach the people who can join you and the people who need what you have) means you'll eventually be surrounded by those who care about your causes. Living and working in this mutually supportive and caring atmosphere is very rewarding and makes life more fun. Giving back will add meaning and power to your life and your experience of yourself.

CONCLUSION

Using *The Ten Smartest Decisions a Woman Can Make After Forty* can help you make the years after forty more satisfying and productive. You have seen how effective they can be in helping you face all the changes that midlife can bring. With these skills, you have the power to bring your dreams of the future into reality. You'll be more aware of the decisions you are making, actively or by default, and will feel confident in your ability to make the best choice.

When you become confident and expert in making mature decisions, decision-making becomes a tool you can apply to every situation in your life. Although this is a time of great change for most women, change need not be upsetting or frightening. Because you know how to decide and re-decide, you'll feel more confident in your ability to shine in new situations. The power to make choices and decisions puts you in charge of your own future. You can use that power to create a life with maximum meaning and maximum effectiveness.

Using your creativity, and giving back from the wisdom you've gained through experience, will enhance your value to others and to yourself. When you use smart decisions and self-awareness to shape your life, it will reflect your deepest aspirations and your fondest dreams. Whatever you choose, if you make smart decisions, the best is yet to come.

BIBLIOGRAPHY

Books

Branden, Nathaniel. *Honoring the Self: Personal Integrity and the Heroic Potentials of Human Nature.* New York: Jeremy P. Tarcher, Inc., 1983.

Brock, Henry S. *Your Complete Guide to Money Happiness.* New York: Legacy Publishing Co., Inc., 1997.

Byrne, Robert. *1,911 Best Things Anybody Ever Said.* New York: Balantine Books, 1988.

Csikszentmihalyi, Mihaly. *Flow: The Psychology of Optimal Experience.* New York: HarperCollins, Inc., 1990.

Dychtwald, Ken. *Age Power: How the Twenty-First Century Will Be Ruled by the New Old.* New York: Jeremy P. Tarcher, Inc., 1999.

Hay, Louise. *You Can Heal Your Life.* Carlsbad, CA: Hay House, 1984.

Hayes, Christopher, and Kate Kelly. *Money Makeovers: How Women Can Control Their Financial Destiny.* New York: Doubleday, 1998.

Hoff, Benjamin. *The Tao of Pooh.* New York: Viking Penguin USA, 1982.

Isaacs, Florence. *Toxic Friends, True Friends.* New York: William Morrow & Co., 1999.

Jibrin, Janis. *The Unofficial Guide to Dieting Safely.* Foster City, CA: IDG Books Worldwide, Inc., 1998.

Katz, Lawrence C., and Manning Rubin. *Keep Your Brain Alive: 83 Neurobic Exercises to Help Prevent Memory Loss and Increase Mental Fitness.* New York: Workman Publishing, 1999.

Larson, William. *No More 9 to 5: What to Do When You Can't Find a Job, Don't Want a Job, or Are Unhappy with the Job You Have.* Bellingham, WA: Life Success Systems, 1985.

Milano, Carol. *Hers: The Wise Woman's Guide to Starting a Business on $2,000 or Less.* New York: Allworth Press, 1997.

Moore, Thomas. *Care of the Soul.* New York: HarperCollins, Inc., 1998.

Nelson, Miriam. *Strong Women Stay Young.* New York: Bantam Books, 1999.

Ornish, Dean, M.D. *Love and Survival: The Scientific Basis for the Healing Power of Intimacy.* New York: HarperCollins, Inc., 1998.

Perry, Susan K. *Writing in Flow: Keys to Enhanced Creativity.* Cincinnati, OH: Writer's Digest Books, 1999.

Podiasek, Jill. *The Ten Habits of Naturally Slim People.* Lincolnwood, IL: Contemporary Books, Inc., 1997.

Roche, Lorin. *Meditation Made Easy.* San Francisco: HarperSanFrancisco, 1998.

Roizen, Michael. *Real Age: Are You as Young as You Can Be?* New York: HarperCollins, Inc., 1999.

Roth, Geneen. *When You Eat at the Refrigerator, Pull up a Chair.* New York: Hyperion, 1998.

The Quotable Woman. Philadelphia: Running Press Book Publishers, 1991.

Siegel, Bernie, M.D. *Peace, Love and Healing.* New York: Harper & Row, 1989.

Sinetar, Marsha. *Elegant Choices, Healing Choices: Finding Grace and Wholeness in Everything We Choose.* Mahwah, NJ: Paulist Press, 1989.

———. *Ordinary People as Monks and Mystics.* Mahwah, NJ: Paulist Press, 1986.

Skog, Susan. *ABC's for Living.* Deerfield Beach, FL: Health Communications, Inc., 1997.

Stephens, Autumn. *Untamed Tongues.* Berkeley, CA: Conari Press, 1993.

Periodicals

Clark, Kim. 2000. The New Midlife. *U.S. News & World Report.* March, 70.

Epstein, Robert. 2000. Stress Busters. *Psychology Today.* March–April, vol. 33, no. 2, 30.

Heyn, Dalma. 1995. Why Girls Don't Wanna Have Fun. *New Woman.* June, 86.

Parris, Jennifer. 1998. Career and Money News. *New Woman.* January, 91.

Putnam, Carol. 1985. My Selves in the Mirror. *In Context.* Summer, 27.

St. George, Michele. 2000. Practice Makes Imperfect. *Mature Outlook.* April, vol. 17, no. 2, 66.

Ubell, Earl. 1987. Eat Wiser, Live Longer. *Parade.* 25, October, 16.

United States Government. 1999. National Vital Statistics Report. 13, December, vol. 47, no. 28.

White, Sabina. 1993. Laughter Workshops. *Omni.* October, 38.

The Internet

RealAge.com. "Cut Your Credit." RealAge Tip of the Day, April 28, 2000.

RealAge.com. "Grey Matters." RealAge Tip of the Day, March 24, 2000.

RealAge.com. "Laughter Is Serious Medicine." RealAge Tip of the Day, May 3, 2000.

RealAge.com. "Soothe Stress for a Song." RealAge Tip of the Day, February 18, 2000.

RealAge.com. "Volunteer for Vitality." RealAge Tip of the Day, October 17, 2000.

Saluter, Arlene, and Terry Lugaila. "Current Population Reports, Population Characteristics," Bureau of the Census Web site: www.census.org.1996.

Winfrey, Oprah. "When Fortune Smiles." *The Utne Reader.* May–June 2000, from the Web site www.zukav.com (Soul guest: Oprah Winfrey, Inner Revolution).

APPENDIX

Resources for Further Exploration

This appendix will help you find some useful resources and organizations. It is only a partial listing; your local library and the Internet offer many more avenues to explore. Books, organizations, and Internet sources are listed by chapter. Any books that were referenced within the text are also listed by author in the bibliography.

Chapter 1

Books About Decision-making

Branden, Nathaniel. *Honoring the Self: Personal Integrity and the Heroic Potentials of Human Nature.* New York: Jeremy P. Tarcher, Inc., 1983.

Cappacchione, Lucia. *The Creative Journal.* North Hollywood, CA: Newcastle Publishing Co., 1989.

Gershon, David, and Gail Straub. *Empowerment: The Art of Creating Your Life as You Want It.* New York: Delta Books, 1991.

Hay, Louise. *You Can Heal Your Life.* Carlsbad, CA: Hay House, 1984.

Roberts, Denton. *Able and Equal.* Culver City, CA: Human Esteem Publishing, 1984.

―――. *Find Purpose, Find Power.* Culver City, CA: Human Esteem Publishing, 1997.

Tessina, Tina. *The Real Thirteenth Step: Discovering Confidence, Self-Reliance and Autonomy Beyond the Twelve-Step Programs.* 2nd Ed. Franklin Lakes, NJ: Career Press, 2001.

Tessina, Tina, with Elizabeth Friar Williams. *The 10 Smartest Decisions a Woman Can Make Before 40.* Deerfield Beach, FL: Health Communications, Inc., 1998.

Chapter 2

Books About Changing Roles

Ries, Shauna, and Genna Murphy. *Quality of Life: How to Get It, How to Keep It.* New York: William Morrow & Co., 1999.

Sinetar, Marsha. *Elegant Choices, Healing Choices: Finding Grace and Wholeness in Everything We Choose.* Mahwah, NJ: Paulist Press, 1989.

Smith, Riley K., and Tina Tessina. *How to Be a Couple and Still Be Free.* Second edition. North Hollywood, CA: Newcastle Publishing Co., 1987.

Tessina, Tina. *The Unofficial Guide to Dating Again.* Foster City, CA: IDG Books Worldwide, Inc., 1999.

Resources for Changing Roles and Family Issues

Alcoholics Anonymous
AA World Services
P.O. Box 459, Grand Central Station
New York, NY 10163
212-870-3400
www.aa.org

American Association of Marriage and Family Therapy (AAMFT)
1133 15th Street NW, Suite 300
Washington, DC 20005-2710
202-452-0109
www.aamft.org

American Association of Retired Persons (AARP)
Membership Communications
601 E Street NW
Washington, DC 20049
800-424-3410
www.aarp.org

The Association for Humanistic Psychology
45 Franklin Street, Suite 315
San Francisco, CA 94102
415-864-8850
www.ahpweb.org

The Therapist Finder of the California Association of Marriage Family Therapists
www.camft.org/

Chapter 3

Books About Revitalizing Your Career

Helgesen, Sally. *Everyday Revolutionaries: Working Women and the Transformation of American Life.* New York: Doubleday, 1998.

Larson, William. *No More 9 to 5: What to Do When You Can't Find a Job, Don't Want a Job, or Are Unhappy with the Job You Have*. Bellingham, WA: Life Success Systems, 1985.

Milano, Carol. *Hers: The Wise Woman's Guide to Starting a Business on $2,000 or Less*. New York: Allworth Press, 1997.

Unger, Harlow G. *But What If I Don't Want to Go to College?—A Guide to Success Through Alternative Education*. New York: Facts on File, Inc., 1992.

Web Sites for Business Owners

Marketplace for Women in Business
www.bizwomen.com

Small Business Administration
www.sbaonline.sba.gov/womeninbusiness

Smart Business Supersite
www.smartbiz.com

Women's Bureau Clearing House, Department of Labor
202-219-4486 (answers questions about workplace issues)

Women's Franchise Network of the International Franchise Association
www.francise.org/wfn

Chapter 4

Books That Focus on Friendship

Goodman, Ellen, and Patricia O'Brien. *I Know Just What You Mean: The Power of Friendship in Women's Lives*. New York: Simon & Schuster, 2000.

Hopke, Robert H., and Laura Rafaty. *A Couple of Friends*. Berkeley, CA: Wildcat Canyon Press, 1999.

Isaacs, Florence. *Toxic Friends, True Friends*. New York: William Morrow & Co., 1999.

Ornish, Dean, M.D. *Love and Survival: The Scientific Basis for the Healing Power of Intimacy*. New York: HarperCollins, Inc., 1998.

Chapter 5

Books About Staying Healthy

Broadhurst, Judith. *The Women's Guide to Online Services.* New York: McGraw-Hill, Inc., 1995.

Jibrin, Janis. *The Unofficial Guide to Dieting Safely.* Foster City, CA: IDG Books Worldwide, Inc., 1998.

Katz, Lawrence C., and Manning Rubin. *Keep Your Brain Alive: 83 Neurobic Exercises to Help Prevent Memory Loss and Increase Mental Fitness.* New York: Workman Publishing, 1999.

Langer, Ellen. *Mindfulness.* New York: Addison-Wesley Publishing Co., 1989.

Nelson, Miriam. *Strong Women Stay Young.* New York: Bantam Books, 1999.

Podiasek, Jill. *The Ten Habits of Naturally Slim People.* Lincolnwood, IL: Contemporary Books, Inc., 1997.

Roizen, Michael. *Real Age: Are You as Young as You Can Be?* New York: HarperCollins, Inc., 1999.

Roth, Geneen. *When You Eat at the Refrigerator, Pull up a Chair.* New York: Hyperion, 1998.

Weil, Andrew, M.D. *Spontaneous Healing.* New York: Alfred A. Knopf, Inc., 1995.

Magazines on Health

Yoga Journal
2054 University Avenue, Suite 600
Berkeley, CA 94704
510-841-9200
www.yogajournal.com (for a list of certified yoga teachers)

Chapter 6

Books About Financial Security

Beardstown Ladies Investment Club with Leslie Whitaker. *The Beardstown Ladies Commonsense Investment Guide: How We Beat the Stock Market—And How You Can Too.* New York: Hyperion, 1995.

Benke, William, and Joseph Fowler. *All About Real Estate Investing: From the Inside Out.* New York: McGraw-Hill, Inc., 1995.

Brock, Henry S. *Your Complete Guide to Money Happiness.* New York: Legacy, 1997.

Detweiler, Gerri. *The Ultimate Credit Handbook.* New York: Putnam-Berkley Group Inc., 1997.

Hayes, Christopher, and Kate Kelly. *Money Makeovers: How Women Can Control Their Financial Destiny.* New York: Doubleday, 1998.

Pivar, William H. *Real Estate Investing from A to Z: The Most Comprehensive, Practical, and Readable Guide to Investing Profitably in Real Estate.* New York: McGraw-Hill, Inc., 1997.

Stanny, Barbara. *Prince Charming Isn't Coming: How Women Get Smart About Money.* New York: Viking Penguin USA, 1997.

Tobias, Andrew P. *The Only Investment Guide You'll Ever Need.* Harvest Books, 1999.

Business Magazines

Barron's National Business Weekly, subscriptions
200 Burnett Road
Chicopee, MA 01020

BottomLine Personal (an investment advice newsletter), subscriptions
P.O. Box 58446
Boulder, CO 80322

Investor's Business Daily, subscriptions
12655 Beatrice Street
Los Angeles, CA 90066
www.investors.com

Financial Resources

American Consumer Credit Counselors (non-profit counseling for financial recovery)
24 Crescent Street
Waltham, MA 02154
781-647-3377
www.consumercredit.com

Institute of Certified Financial Planners
7600 East Eastman Avenue, Suite 301
Denver, CO 80231-4397
303-751-7600

National Association of Investment Counselors
Support and Services Office
120 W. 12th Street, Suite 1100
Kansas City, MO 64105-1925
www.naic.org

National Association of Securities Dealers
1390 Piccard Drive
Rockville, MD 20850-3389
800-289-9999
www.nasdr.com

Chapter 7

Books About Personal Transformation

Alter, Robert, and Jane Alter. *The Transformative Power of Crisis*. New York: Harper-Collins, Inc., 2000.

Cameron, Julia, and Mark Bryan. *The Artist's Way*. New York: Jeremy P. Tarcher, Inc., 1995.

Campbell, Joseph, with Bill Moyers. *The Power of Myth*. New York: Doubleday, 1988.

Csikszentmihalyi, Mihaly. *Creativity: Flow and the Psychology of Discovery and Invention*. New York: HarperCollins, Inc., 1996.

————. *The Evolving Self: A Psychology for the Third Millennium*. New York: Harper-Collins, Inc., 1993.

Hillman, James. *The Soul's Code: In Search of Character and Calling*. New York: Random House, Inc., 1996.

Perry, Susan K. *Writing in Flow: Keys to Enhanced Creativity*. Cincinnati, OH: Writer's Digest Books, 1999.

Siegel, Bernie, M.D. *Peace, Love and Healing*. New York: Harper & Row, 1989.

Wilbur, Ken. *A Brief History of Everything*. Boston: Shambhala Publications, Inc., 1996.

Chapter 8

Books About Having Fun

Csikszentmihalyi, Mihaly. *Flow: The Psychology of Optimal Experience.* New York: Harper-Collins, Inc., 1990.

Golden, Pamela. *Choose the Happiness Habit.* New York: Roedway Press, 1998.

Hoff, Benjamin. *The Tao of Pooh.* New York: Viking Penguin USA, 1982.

Jackowski, Karol. *101 Fun Things to Do Before You Die.* Notre Dame, IN: Ave Maria Press, 1989.

Seligman, Martin E. P. *Learned Optimism.* New York: Alfred A. Knopf, Inc., 1991.

Chapter 9

Books About Finding Meaning

Altea, Rosemary. *You Own the Power.* New York: William Morrow & Co., 2000.

Leder, Drew, M.D. *Spiritual Passages: Embracing Life's Sacred Journey.* New York: Jeremy P. Tarcher, Inc., 1997.

Peck, M. Scott. *The Road Less Traveled.* New York: Simon & Schuster, Inc., 1985.

———. *Further Along the Road Less Traveled.* New York: Simon & Schuster, Inc., 1993.

Roche, Lorin. *Meditation Made Easy.* San Francisco: HarperSanFrancisco, 1998.

Sinetar, Marsha. *Ordinary People as Monks and Mystics.* Mahwah, NJ: Paulist Press, 1986.

Williamson, Maryanne. *Illuminata.* New York: Random House, Inc., 1994.

Magazines Devoted to Spirituality

Parabola: The Magazine of Myth and Tradition
(Joseph Campbell began this wonderful spiritual study guide), subscriptions
656 Broadway
New York, NY 10012-9824

Chapter 10

Books About Giving Back

Elgin, Duane. *Voluntary Simplicity.* New York: William Morrow & Co., 1981.

Moore, Thomas. *Care of the Soul.* New York: HarperCollins, Inc., 1998.

Organizations for Giving Back

American Association of University Women
1111 16th Street NW
Washington, DC 20036
800-326-AAUW
www.aauw.org

American Mensa
201 Main Street, Suite 1101
Fort Worth, TX 75102
817-332-2600
www.mensa.org

League of Women Voters
1730 M Street NW
Washington, DC 20036-4508
202-429-1965
www.lwv.org

Search Engines on the Internet, for Further Assistance

AltaVista: www.altavista.digital.com

Excite: www.excite.com

Infoseek: www.infoseek.com

Lycos: www.lycos.com

Yahoo: www.yahoo.com

Telephone Books on the Internet

Locate a business at www.yellowpages.com

Find a person at www.switchboard.com

Bookstores on the Internet

Amazon Books: www.amazon.com

The Bodhi Tree: www.bodhitree.com

Crown Books: www.crownbooks.com/

The Tattered Cover: www.tatteredcover.com/tc

INDEX

ABOUT THE AUTHOR

Tina B. Tessina, Ph.D., L.M.F.T., has twenty-five years of experience as a licensed marriage and family therapist. She is the author of ten books, including *The Unofficial Guide to Dating Again* (1999); *The 10 Smartest Decisions a Woman Can Make Before 40* (1998); *The Real Thirteenth Step: Discovering Confidence, Self-Reliance and Autonomy Beyond the Twelve-Step Programs* (1991); *Gay Relationships: How to Find Them, How to Improve Them, How to Make Them Last* (1989); and *Lovestyles: How to Celebrate Your Differences* (1987).

Dr. Tessina co-authored, with Riley K. Smith, *How to Be a Couple and Still Be Free* (1980), *True Partners: A Workbook for Developing Lasting Intimacy* (1992), and *Equal Partners* (1994).

Dr. Tessina lectures and conducts nationwide workshops on all of her books and has appeared on major television and radio shows, including *Donohue, Oprah, Geraldo,* and *Larry King Live.* She lives in Long Beach, California, with her husband, Richard Sharrard.

To reach Dr. Tessina for questions, lectures, workshops, and individual and couple therapy:

Tina B. Tessina, Ph.D., L.M.F.T.
License MX 13629
P.O. Box 4883
Long Beach, CA 90804

562-438-8077

Web site: www.tinatessina.com
e-mail: tinatessina@compuserve.com